Peter de Figueiredo and Jul

111 Places
in Liverpool
That You
Shouldn't
Miss

111

emons:

All photographs © Peter de Figueiredo except: Active Learning Laboratory,
Holt's Arcade, John Lewis Pedestrian Bridge, Mathew Street on Saturday Night,
Philharmonic Dining Rooms, Port of Liverpool Building: © Patrick M. Higgins
Photography; Angel Field: © Andy Thomson, BCA; Burne-Jones Windows:
© Historic England; Chambré Hardman's Kitchen: © Cavendish Press;
Della Robbia Room: Philip Eastwood, © Williamson Museum and Art Gallery;
Loophonium: © David Tomlinson; The Music Room: © Mark McNulty, courtesy
of Liverpool Philharmonic; The Portrait Wall: © Helene Binet, courtesy Haworth
Tompkins; Queensway Tunnel: © Stuart Rayner, courtesy of Merseytravel;
Salammbo: © Mark McNulty, courtesy of National Museums Liverpool;
Town Hall: © Liverpool City Council; Williamson Tunnels: © Chris Iles, Friends
of Williamsons Tunnels; World Cultures Gallery: © National Museums Liverpool
Design: Eva Kraskes, based on a design
by Lübbeke | Naumann | Thoben
Edited by Katrina Fried
Maps: altancicek.design, www.altancicek.de
Printing and binding: B.O.S.S Medien GmbH, Goch
Printed in Germany 2016
ISBN 978-3-95451-769-5
First edition

Did you enjoy it? Do you want more?
Join us in uncovering new places around the world on:
www.111places.com

Foreword

Liverpool is a small city with a big history. Historic architecture, sporting events, museums and galleries, and the city's world-famous musical and theatrical heritage have all contributed to its character, but it was the port that gave Liverpool its distinctive cosmopolitan outlook. The mixed population of natives and immigrants created a culture of verbal humour and creativity that singles Liverpool out from other British cities. Liverpool is not genteel or understated. When it is grand it is very grand, when it is poor it is very poor, and when it is original it is inimitable.

Liverpool's recent history has been unhappy, its fabric hit by the blitz, its economy decimated by changes in global trade, and its people often ill served by local politicians. But it is a resilient city. In the 1990s it began to rediscover its pride; warehouse conversions and new apartment blocks encouraged city-centre living, and neglected historic buildings were restored. The year 2008 was the annus mirabilis, when Liverpool was European Capital of Culture, and the Liverpool One retail zone opened. Both attracted millions, locals and visitors alike, and stimulated a revival. Cruise liners began to return to the Pier Head. Boutique hotels, good restaurants, artisan bakeries, and coffee houses blossomed in previously down-at-heel areas such as Bold Street and RopeWalks. The city's famous pub culture was supplemented by stylish cocktail bars, and a new creative quarter emerged in the still edgy Baltic Triangle. Even written-off areas such as Granby Street are fighting back.

All this has given us plenty of material to choose from. Our selection is personal, led by a shared taste for the quirky, which has taken us to some offbeat places; but it has also led us to neglected corners of classic Liverpool attractions such as the two cathedrals, the museums, the magnificent cultural quarter, and the peerless waterfront. We hope you have as much fun exploring this book as we have had writing it.

111 Places

1 10 Rumford Place

Smuggling and espionage in the American Civil War

This pleasingly modest brick building was the headquarters of a covert operation during the American Civil War to support the Confederates in defiance of official British neutrality. The oldest part is the 1830s Georgian-style frontage in the second courtyard, the only surviving example of an early office building in central Liverpool. This was the address of Fraser, Trenholm and Co, the British arm of a shipping firm based in Charleston, South Carolina. When, in 1861, the Union began the blockade of the Confederate ports in the South, the company drastically changed direction. It became the unofficial European banker for the Confederates and began to break the blockade, running goods to the South and smuggling cotton out.

James Bulloch, a Confederate agent, arrived in Liverpool in 1861 and went to 10 Rumford Place with a shopping list that included pistols, warships, and 4,000 pairs of flannel drawers. The Confederacy had no fleet and no access to supplies because of the blockade. Through Bulloch, orders were placed with Merseyside shipyards for the *Florida*, built by Miller and Sons in Toxteth, and the *Alabama*, built by Laird in Birkenhead. Both were spirited out of Liverpool, and inflicted great damage on Union vessels, although, due to espionage carried out for the American consul in Liverpool, two ram ships built by Laird for the Confederates were seized by the British government.

Liverpool also had a curious role in the ending of the Civil War, usually said to have been on April 9, 1865, when the Confederate general Robert E. Lee surrendered to the Unionist general Ulysses S. Grant at Appomattox, Virginia. The war actually ended in Liverpool seven months later. The Confederate ship *Shenandoah* had been at sea and unaware of Lee's surrender. It sailed into Liverpool and it was in the Mersey on November 6 that the Confederate flag was lowered for the last time.

Address 10 Rumford Place, Liverpool L3 9DG | **Getting there** 5-minute walk from James Street station | **Tip** Round the corner on Chapel Street is Liverpool Parish Church, dedicated to Our Lady and St Nicholas, patron saint of sailors. Known as the Seamen's Church, it has a weathervane in the form of a ship.

2__69A

Browse for curios in an Aladdin's cave

The long, narrow interior feels like a slightly musty souk, piled high with bric-a-brac of all kinds – antiques, collectibles, Asian art, kitchenalia, vintage clothing, and good old junk, displayed on a jumble of shelves, ledges, and tables or in vitrines, interspersed with straggly houseplants and potted palms. There are extraordinary, fascinating, rare, and useless objects everywhere: clockwork toys, Soviet porcelain, a copy of *Ken Dodd's Diddymen Annual*, a bit of famille rose, a Korean figurine, Murano glass, suitcases with old luggage labels, Art Deco scent bottles … As you progress further into the shop, past the racks of clothes, and hats – including an unusually large collection of cream and beige corduroy jackets, towards the vinyl and books at the back, you regress into a dreamlike state, induced by the sound of ambient music and the faint smell of incense. While you browse, you'll discover things you haven't seen since your childhood – a pair of 1960s nylons, a chunky 1950s white telephone – or things you have never seen at all, such as a pair of lavender bags made to look like tiny ballet shoes.

As the owner Trevor explains, the shop was not planned, it just evolved. He started out selling 20th-century decorative art and vintage clothing in Birmingham in 1976, moved to Liverpool to a stall in the legendary Aunt Twacky's Bazaar in Mathew Street, and in 1977, opened a shop in Renshaw Street. This is his third shop in the same street; the tall, narrow Arts and Crafts frontage was formerly Quiggins Marine and Architectural Ironmongers, who supplied the *Titanic* and the Liver Building. Although the address is No. 75, he brought the number 69A from his previous shop.

A fixture at 69A is a fat ginger cat called Murdoch. He is usually to be found sleeping in the sun on a ledge near the door, but beware! He is liable to appear from nowhere and leap onto the counter just as you are trying to pay.

Address 75 Renshaw Street, Liverpool L1 2SJ, Tel +44 1517088873, www.69aliverpool.co.uk | **Getting there** 10-minute walk from Lime Street station; 8-minute walk from Central station | **Hours** Daily noon – 6pm | **Tip** Meditation fans will love the Olive Tree (61 Renshaw Street), selling fair-trade products, yoga mats, singing bowls, reiki candles, incense, and essential oils.

3   A Case History

Heaps of luggage scattered on the pavement

Walk along Hope Street, and at the top of Mount Street, you will find an intriguing sculpture, punningly entitled *A Case History*. It was the result of a competition organised by the nearby Liverpool Institute for the Performing Arts. The winner was John King, who had worked with the American architect James Wines on a similar piece at Salford Quays representing barrels, bales, oil drums, and machinery.

The original idea behind the suitcases sculpture was to evoke the arrivals and departures of the people who converged on Liverpool from all over Europe intending to emigrate to America – those who stayed as well as those who were merely passing through. When it was decided to place the work in Hope Street, it was made site specific. It includes a parcel from Penguin Books addressed to The Liverpool Poets (Adrian Henri lived in Mount Street), and another, marked *Fragile*, destined for the Hahnemann Hospital, the first homeopathic hospital in Britain; its building is still on Hope Street. A guitar case with a Concorde flight label to New York has Paul McCartney's name on it; he supplied a real guitar case to be cast by the sculptor. McCartney attended the Liverpool Institute when it was a boys' school. So did George Harrison and the comedian Arthur Askey, also name-checked on luggage labels.

The case labelled *Uncle* is for "Uncle" Kwok Fong, who worked with Asian seamen sailing from Liverpool. There is a suitcase for Josephine Butler, who worked with prostitutes at the workhouse on Brownlow Hill, and one for the activist Margaret Simey, who lived nearby. You will also find labels for John Lennon and Stuart Sutcliffe. Both went to the Liverpool College of Art, which used to be next door to the Institute. *A Case History* conjures up a whole world of fascinating people associated with the area. Perhaps in the future, today's movers and shakers will receive similar recognition.

Address Hope Street, Liverpool L1 9BZ | Getting there 10-minute walk from Central station; CityLink bus from Liverpool One bus station to Hope Street | Tip Nearby, with a colourful Superlambanana outside, is 60 Hope Street, one of Liverpool's best restaurants.

4__Active Learning Laboratory

The colourful world of engineering

Liverpool is famed for its townscape, with well-known landmarks like the Liver Building, Radio City Tower, and the two cathedrals. In 2009, the remodelling of the University of Liverpool's engineering department created a futuristic addition to the city's skyline. The centrepiece is the Active Learning Laboratory, a seven-storey glass box, which appears to hover in the night sky like something from another world, glowing in an endlessly changing sequence of colours. The building, designed by Sheppard Robson and Partners with Arup Lighting, cleverly wraps a new skin of fritted glass panels around the existing columns of a 1960s brutalist tower. The façades are made up of two layers of glass sandwiched together with a dotted pattern imprinted on the outer layer. The translucent dots provide a surface onto which light is reflected from hundreds of LEDs housed inside, creating the glow.

The lighting can be programmed to display simple numbers, letters, and geometric shapes as well as an infinite array of rotating colours and morphing designs and patterns. It has been used to celebrate significant events such as festivals and saints' days; for example, the façades were illuminated in blue to mark World Diabetes Day, raising awareness of the disease and the university's important research into its treatment and cure. For the Liverpool Biennial, artist Paul Rooney created a strange artwork called *He Was Afraid*, consisting of a sequence of international maritime signal flags forming words recalling the unsettling power of the past. At a more functional level, the new, 21st-century structure not only makes an iconic visual statement, but also exploits cutting-edge LED technology and electronic solar tracking equipment to reduce energy consumption and running costs.

Address Brownlow Hill, Liverpool L 69 3GJ, www.liv.ac.uk/engineering | Getting there 12-minute walk from Lime Street station or Central station | Tip On the opposite side of Brownlow Hill is the Liverpool School of Art and Design, another of the city's best contemporary buildings, which frequently holds public events and exhibitions (www.ljmu.ac.uk/about-us/events).

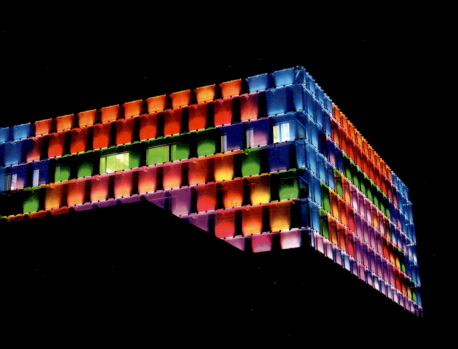

5 Adelphi Hotel

Where Roy Rogers's Trigger took a bow

When the Adelphi opened, in 1914, it was the most luxurious hotel outside London. The grand scale of the present building, larger than its two predecessors on the site, is a testament to Liverpool's importance in early-20th-century transatlantic travel, when its customers were wealthy passengers en route by ship to America. The once elegant rooms have seen better days, but the ghosts of a more glamorous past hover around the public rooms on the ground floor, and in some of the bedrooms that have not been modernised. From the marble entrance hall, a set of steps makes a dramatic approach to the vast top-lit Central Court, which is lined with pink marble pilasters and tall archways opening onto restaurants on each side. Beyond this is the impressive Empire-style Hypostyle Hall.

The Adelphi shot to fame in 1997 with the excruciating reality TV docusoap, *Hotel*, which recorded the back-of-house antics of the unruly staff. It memorably featured an indoor barbecue that smoked out the banqueting hall, leading to acerbic verbal exchanges between the chef and the deputy manager, who coined the famous catch phrase "Just cook will yer."

Many famous guests have stayed at the hotel, including Winston Churchill, Franklin D. Roosevelt, Frank Sinatra, Laurel and Hardy, Judy Garland, and the Beatles. Bob Dylan can be seen waving to his fans from the balcony of his room at the Adelphi in the documentary *Don't Look Back*. The most unusual guest was the cowboy Roy Rogers's horse, Trigger, who visited his master's bedroom on March 8, 1954. Rogers was in bed with the flu and felt too ill to greet his many fans who were gathered outside on Lime Street, so Trigger stood in, rearing up on his hind legs outside the front of the hotel. The celebrity quadruped then mounted the staircase and took a bow from a first-floor window, much to the delight of the onlookers.

Address Ranelagh Place, Liverpool L3 5UL, Tel +44 8712220029, www.britanniahotels.com |
Getting there 5-minute walk from Lime Street station; 3-minute walk from Central station |
Tip The Central Pub, opposite Central station at 31 Ranelagh Street, has an eye-catching
interior lined with Victorian glasswork, mirrors, decorative plasterwork, and panelling.

6 Alma de Cuba

From Latin Mass to Latin-American bar

Alma de Cuba is the outrageous occupant of Liverpool's oldest surviving Roman Catholic church. Dedicated to St Peter, the church opened with a High Mass on September 11, 1788, and served the Catholic community for almost 200 years. The original building, a simple brick box, was later enlarged. The imposing altar, flanked by marble columns with the inscription *Tu es Petrus*, dates from 1898. The church was damaged in the blitz, and after the war, the surrounding area fell into decline. With few people living in the parish, St Peter's closed in 1978 and remained empty for the next 25 years.

Finally the enterprising developer Urban Splash acquired it for conversion to offices, but unable to find tenants, they decided instead to turn the church into a bar and restaurant. The renovation was fraught with difficulties. Not only was the building on the point of collapse, but during construction they found buried in the crypt the remains of Benedictine monks, which had to be re-interred at Ampleforth Abbey.

When Alma de Cuba opened in 2005, it caused a stir amongst some of the Catholic community, for although the church had been deconsecrated, it retained sacred fittings such as the high altar, murals, and memorial tablets. Now they are highlighted with hundreds of flickering candles within the otherwise dark interior, where a Latin-American carnival atmosphere has been created. There is live music with samba dancers most evenings, and on Fridays and Saturdays at 11pm, thousands of rose petals are launched from the balcony onto the revellers below. On Sundays brunch is served to the accompaniment of a gospel choir.

The food also has a Spanish accent, with tapas at lunchtime and brochetta and grills in the evening. A speciality is the Ron Zacapa 23-year-old rum from Guatemala, a headier brew than the sacramental wine that was served in former days.

Address St Peter's Church, Seel Street, Liverpool L1 4BH, Tel +44 8435044692, www.alma-de-cuba.com | Getting there 10-minute walk from Central station | Hours Mon–Thu noon–11pm, Fri–Sat noon–2am, Sun noon–11pm | Tip If you've not yet had enough, try Empire Seel Street (57–59 Seel Street), a club with four individually themed floors, each playing a different type of music.

7 __ Anfield

Tour the stadium, visit the museum, buy the kit

For supporters of the Reds, Anfield is Liverpool's third cathedral, Bill Shankly is God, and Stephen Gerrard is the Keeper of the Relics. You enter the hallowed ground through the Shankly Gates, commemorating the legendary manager (or the Paisley Gates, named after his successor); you are greeted by the Shankly statue ("He Made the People Happy"), and in the museum you can see Gerrard's collection of football shirts, trophies, and memorabilia sanctified by their associations with the world's great players or his team's victories. The display is accompanied by a video of Gerrard, team captain from 2003 to 2015, talking about his treasures. Even if you are not a football fan, a visit to Anfield is essential to understanding a vital part of the city's psychology. And it's not just a local thing: there are millions of supporters all over the world.

Anfield opened for football in 1884. Confusingly, it was first used by Everton FC, but after a rent dispute, the Everton club went to Goodison Park, and in 1892, Liverpool FC was founded, with Anfield as its base. Today the stadium is huge, with seating for more than 50,000. Stadium tours include going behind the scenes; you can even book a VIP experience and meet some of the players; or you can just turn up and visit the Liverpool FC Story, an absorbing interactive museum showcasing the club, its famous players, and its greatest moments, enlivened by videos and the sounds of roaring crowds singing "You'll Never Walk Alone." Among the exhibits are silverware including all five European trophies; a mock-up of the infamous Kop, rebuilt as an all-seater in 1994; and a painting by Adrian Henri commemorating the tragic Hillsborough disaster.

There's a photo booth where you can have your picture taken with a choice of nine different backgrounds; afterwards, you can eat at the Boot Room Sports Cafe; and of course, there is a vast shop with an enormous range of kit.

Address Liverpool FC, Anfield Road, Liverpool L 4 0TH, Tel +44 1512606677, www.liverpoolfc.com | **Getting there** Bus 917 from St John's Lane (match days only); bus 26 or 27 from Liverpool One bus station; bus 17 from Queen Square bus station | **Hours** Museum: Mon–Sun 9am–5pm; tours (advance booking essential) 10am–3pm | **Tip** Across the street, at 199 Oakfield Road, is Home Baked, a community-run co-operative bakery and cafe selling delicious freshly made bread and cakes.

8   Angel Field
An inspiring symbolic garden

Lucky are the students who walk through this outstanding modern garden on the way to classes at Hope University's Creative Campus. Opened in 2010 and designed by Andy Thomson and Becky Sobell of Liverpool-based BCA Landscape, the garden is in four parts, each representing a different phase in Man's spiritual journey.

It starts with Origins, a woodland garden with a bubbling pool, symbolising the primeval beginnings of life. On a circular stone bench are Latin words from St Thomas Aquinas, meaning "Nothing is in the intellect which was not first in the senses." Next is the garden of the Body, an apple orchard in a wildflower meadow, celebrating nature and its fruits, which nurture humankind. The words carved on stone blocks are from *Pied Beauty*, by Gerard Manley Hopkins, a curate of the nearby Church of St Francis Xavier: "Glory be to God for dappled things / For skies of couple colour as a brindled cow." In contrast, the garden of the Mind creates order from untamed nature, with clipped yew hedges and pleached lime trees inspired by Renaissance gardens. Flower beds shaped like Fibonacci spirals and bordered with box hedges are planted with colourful seasonal displays of perennials. In the centre is a circular performance space; across a rill, punctuated by jets of water, is a lawn where people can watch, picnic, or just contemplate. Around the pool is a quotation from Shakespeare's *As You Like It*: "All the world's a stage / And all the men and women merely players."

From Mind one passes to Soul: high above stands an angel on a column, created by sculptor Lucy Glendinning, with lines from Daniel inlaid into the paving below: "He gives wisdom to the wise and knowledge to the discerning. He knows what lies in darkness, and light dwells with him." At night the garden is transformed by discreet lighting into a place of mystery and the angel glows pink from within.

Address Shaw Street, Liverpool L 6 1HP, Tel +44 1512193000 | **Getting there** 20-minute walk from Lime Street station; buses from Queen Square bus station: bus 21 to Everton, Brunswick Road; bus 12 or 13 to Shaw Street; enter via the lodge on Shaw Street | **Hours** 24/7 | **Tip** Musicians Pete Best and Holly Johnson, comedian Ted Ray, and actor Leonard Rossiter were all educated at the Collegiate School on the other side of Shaw Street, later converted to award-winning apartments by Urban Splash.

9 Another Place

The iron men on Crosby Beach

Three kilometres of coastline have been transformed into an unforgettable work of art by Antony Gormley, comprising 100 cast-iron, life-size figures of men, some on the beach, others almost a kilometre out to sea.

Every time you visit, the sculptures look different: they are affected by the tide, the light, the wind, and the weather. Over time, they have changed colour and texture: some are reddened by rust, others are stained with emerald-green seaweed or encrusted with barnacles. Many are partially buried in drifts of sand; at high tide those furthest from the shore become gradually submerged so that they stand up to their necks in water. Each of them faces away from land: whether standing in calm waters or surrounded by crashing breakers, they are stock still, gazing far out to sea.

Each figure is taken from a cast of Gormley's body, but they are not self-portraits or statues in the conventional sense, and they are not elevated on pedestals. They are nameless and empty, waiting for the thoughts and feelings of their viewers; sometimes they look lonely and vulnerable, sometimes steadfast; they are migrants thinking of their homeland, or emigrants dreaming of a new world; they are the spirits of those lost at sea, or the exploited cockle-pickers of Morecambe Bay; they are staring at the offshore wind farm or contemplating our place in the cosmos.

Intended as a temporary installation, they were shown in Germany, Norway, and Belgium before coming to Crosby, where they have found a permanent home. People treat them with affection, dressing them in hats, T-shirts, and sunglasses. Local students of fashion design even put them in period costume. Gormley is delighted by the variety of responses, but even he might have been surprised at the biologists of Liverpool University who surveyed them for a research project about the spread of invasive species of barnacles.

Address Crosby Beach L23 | **Getting there** 6-minute walk from Hall Road station or Blundellsands & Crosby station; 15-minute walk from Waterloo station. Car parks at Hall Road L23 8SY, Crosby Leisure Centre L23 6SX, and Crosby Marine Lake L22 1RR. | **Tip** Between the Marine Lake and Waterloo station, the pretty seafront houses on Beach Lawn, Adelaide Terrace, Marine Crescent, and Marine Terrace have interesting stucco façades and cast-iron verandas.

10__ The Art School Restaurant

Raising the bar for Merseyside dining

The dining room at the Art School Restaurant must be the most beautiful place to eat on Merseyside. It was previously the sculpture room of the School of Art and by day is flooded with light from the glass roof lantern. The well-spaced tables have crisp white tablecloths, the chairs are bright scarlet, and through a glazed slot in the slate-faced wall, you can see the white-hatted brigade at work in the kitchen.

The building was once a large private house, and was then later converted into a home for destitute children, before being used for art education. At the door, you are greeted by the bowler-hatted concierge, who ushers you into an anteroom – part hip cocktail bar with yellow bar stools, part gentlemen's club with armchairs by a wood-burning stove. The tone is set: contemporary cool meets traditional English understatement, combined with impeccable service and food of an extremely high standard.

You will find local ingredients, such as breast of Northop wood pigeon or Rhug Estate venison, served with carefully balanced accompaniments: the pigeon comes with damson purée and beetroot in balsamic, parsnip, and sage, and the trolley of English cheeses includes quince and truffle-scented Liverpool Two Cathedrals honey. The pressed gateau of Provençal vegetables and feta with black-olive dressing is impressive. The prix fixe menu, at lunchtime or early evening, is an outstanding value; more expensive are the "menu excellence" and the tasting menus. Overall, the style is sophisticated but not gimmicky.

Ebullient chef patron Paul Askew, formerly of the acclaimed London Carriage Works, is up there with the greats as a fellow of Britain's Royal Academy of Culinary Arts. The Art School fulfils his long-held dream of creating a top-quality restaurant in Liverpool, set to rival Mayfair fine dining. Some say Askew is aiming too high for Liverpool, but why shouldn't we have the best?

Address 1 Sugnall Street, Liverpool L 7 7EB, Tel +44 1512308600, www.theartschoolrestaurant.co.uk | **Getting there** 15-minute walk from Central station; CityLink or bus 75, 80, 80A, 86, 86A or 86C from Liverpool One bus station | **Hours** Tue–Sat noon–2:15pm, 6:30pm–9:30pm; booking essential | **Tip** Nearby is Blackburne House, formerly a private residence, then a girls' school, and now a thriving women's social-enterprise centre offering education and training, a nursery, a health suite, and a cafe.

11__Baltic Bakehouse

The quest for the perfect loaf

It all started when Chalklin's, the last of the traditional bakeries in Liverpool, closed down. All you could get was factory-made bread from supermarkets and chains. So Sam Henley took down a dusty cookery book from his mother's bookshelves and had a go at making a loaf himself. He was hooked: "You start by trying a simple white loaf with an old bag of flour and next thing you know it's two in the morning and you're arguing about sourdough on an Internet bread forum. The more you learn, the more you want to know." With his sister Grace he started the Baltic Bakehouse in 2013 and it is now one of the success stories of the Baltic Triangle.

Every day except Monday, when the bakery is closed, you can buy the delicious bread – traditional yeasted loaves or tasty sourdoughs – and also great sticky buns, tarts, and doughnuts. There are always different varieties to try – a chart on the website lists which day each kind is on sale. "Baltic Wild," Sam's standard white sourdough, is one of the most popular, available every day and full of flavour and texture without being at all heavy. It takes at least 36 hours from the first mixing to the finished loaf; the more complex-tasting breads can take as long as 72 hours. Sam and his team also do wholemeal, granary, and rye breads, proper baguettes, and ciabattas. Sometimes there are specials such as garlic leaven bread or oat porridge loaf. But don't get there too late, or the bread may have sold out.

The shop, with its sacks of organic flour piled up on one side, is also a small cafe. It's a great place for a breakfast of homemade granola followed by a bacon butty and coffee. Every table is equipped with a toaster, so you can make your own toast and spread it with peanut butter, marmite, jam, or marmalade. For lunch there are soups, salads, and sourdough sandwiches. Sit and watch the ovens in use at the back of the shop and be thankful for places like this, and for the simple pleasures of good bread.

Address 46 Bridgewater Street, Liverpool L1 0AY, Tel +44 1517086686, also at Furrow Cafe, 97 Allerton Road, Liverpool L18 2DD, www.balticbakehouse.co.uk | **Getting there** 15-minute walk from Central station; buses from Liverpool One bus station: CityLink to Jamaica Street; 27 to Sparling Street | **Hours** Tue–Fri 9am–5pm, Sat–Sun 10am–4pm | **Tip** The Lantern Theatre, in a converted warehouse (57 Blundell Street), is an intimate open-plan venue showcasing new talent in fringe theatre, music, and comedy.

12 Baltic Triangle

Where Liverpool's creatives work and play

The Baltic Triangle, a gritty inner-city zone of old warehouses, semi-derelict workshops, and vacant sites, has taken off as the most exciting area in Liverpool.

It all started with the restoration of factories in Greenland Street for the fledgling Liverpool Biennial. Eventually the Biennial office moved into a nearby unit, and the buildings morphed into Camp and Furnace (see p. 31). Now hip outfits such as digital animators Milky Tea; Iron Bird, specialists in aerial cinematography; and Apposing, creators of phone apps, have moved in along with assorted architects, photographers, designers, filmmakers, musicians, and entrepreneurs. Many have set up shop in new workspaces, such as Basecamp and Elevator Studios, which have communal areas for creative networking. Even the Victorian warehouse complex – which used to be known as the Buddleia Building because of the forest of weeds sprouting from its gutters – has been rescued; besides Elevator Studios, its occupants include Liverpool Life Sciences, part of the North Liverpool Academy, along with Giant Bike Store and the Baltic Social.

With these developments have come new cafes such as Coffee and Fandisha, Siren, Unit 51, and the Indian restaurant Balle Balle. There are also event venues like Constellations, with its urban garden, studios, gallery, and cafe-bar, and pop-ups including the Botanical Garden, a summer-only al fresco cocktail bar, next door to the New Bird Skatepark. In the evenings, the New Bird Warehouse, District, and the Garage attract crowds of clubbers.

History can be read in the street names: Greenland Street for the whaling ships, Jamaica Street for sugar and slaves – also commemorated in Blundell Street and New Bird Street, named after slave traders Bryan Blundell and Joseph Bird.

But you don't go to the Baltic Triangle for its past, you go because it's where it's happening now.

Address South of Liverpool One, between Wapping, Park Lane, and Hill Street, Liverpool L1 0BW, www.liverpoolbaltictriangle.co.uk | **Getting there** 10-minute walk from Liverpool One bus station | **Tip** The Swedish Seamen's Church (138 Park Lane) organises everything from Nordic knitting sessions and language classes to Scandinavian film nights (www.nordicliverpool.co.uk).

13___Bascule Bridge
Seesaw in dockland

The word *bascule* comes from the French for seesaw, a device which works on the principle of counterbalance. This is how the bascule bridge across the passage leading into the Stanley Dock used to operate, when it was still working.

Liverpool's seven miles of historic dockland used to rely on a complex system of interlinked docks, where several water bodies might be served by a single maritime entrance, allowing the free movement of ships to different quaysides once they were clear of the tides. With ever-increasing levels of trade and the comings and goings of vessels, it required a multitude of moveable bridges to allow the steam trains, horse-drawn carts, sailors, stevedores, merchants, and customs officials to travel throughout the dockland area. The majority were iron swing bridges, but the most remarkable is the bascule bridge, one of five constructed by the Dock Board in 1932.

The bridge requires little power, for the weight of the roadway is balanced by a ballast tank filled with iron and concrete, and is raised by means of a rack and pinion. When the bridge was built, the country was in the depths of the Great Depression, and the cost of the work was subsidised by unemployment relief. Originally the bridge was operated by hydraulic power, a pressurised water system, which was employed throughout the docks for items with moving parts such as lock gates, capstans, hoists, and cranes, as well as for bridges. The hydraulic engine house that served the bascule bridge is the nearby castellated tower, which is a landmark on the edge of the Stanley Dock. Storage accumulators within the tower were pumped full to provide a constant supply of pressurised water. Although hydraulic power was replaced by electric motors in the 1950s, the original machinery for the bridge remains in place, inside the quaint timber-clad engine room, which spans the roadway on a steel deck.

Address Regent Road, Liverpool L 3 0AN | **Getting there** 20-minute walk from Pier Head; bus 101 from Queen's Square bus station to Stanley Dock | **Tip** Visit the Titanic Hotel, a converted warehouse at the Stanley Dock for coffee or cocktails on the quayside, with a good view of the bridge.

14__Berry and Rye

Secret speakeasy with classic cocktails

"No bookings, just turn up," it says on Twitter. But when you get to 48 Berry Street, there's nothing there – no signs – just two shabby black doors, and no clue as to which, if either, is the right one. You hang about on the pavement for a bit, feeling anxious. Eventually a door opens, a bouncer emerges, and tells you how long you have to wait (best not to go on a Saturday night). After a while, a few people come out and the bouncer reappears; you are whisked inside the thick black curtains and suddenly you relax.

Berry and Rye is usually crowded but it is the opposite of frantic: you could even call it cosy. It is not very large and the tables are tightly spaced, but there is no loud music, only gently wailing jazz or blues – it might be Billie Holiday or Muddy Waters. The lighting is soft; there are candles stuck into bottles on the tables, bare brick walls, distressed wallpaper, wooden pews and settles, an old piano, and a Victorian fireplace. Sit down – service is at table, a rarity these days – and water appears at once. A pile of second-hand books turns out to be the menus, inlaid within a bizarre selection of well-thumbed volumes including *The Wizard of Oz* and *Cheshire: The Biography of Leonard Cheshire, VC, OM.*

Berry and Rye specialises in classic whisky and gin cocktails, juleps, and cobblers: the menu lists four different manhattans, several martinis, and evergreen classics such as negronis and bloody marys. The servers are casually dressed but they know their stuff, and are able to advise the novice as well as debate with the connoisseur the nuances of the hundreds of whiskies on display behind the bar. To line the stomach you can order a platter of well-chosen cheeses or some olives with good bread from the Baltic Bakehouse (see p. 30). Cocktail bars are everywhere these days, but serious expertise and attention to detail mark out Berry and Rye – if you can find it.

Address 48 Berry Street, Liverpool L1 4JQ, Twitter: @berry_and_rye (no phone number or website) | **Getting there** 7-minute walk from Central station | **Hours** Sun–Thu 5pm–2am, Fri–Sat 4pm–3am | **Tip** Some Place, an absinthe bar under the same management, is around the corner at 43 Seel Street (also unmarked, upstairs from the Zanzibar).

15_Bidston Hill

A windmill, an observatory, and a lighthouse

If you want a breather from the city, head for Bidston Hill, 100 acres of wild heath and woodland, only about five kilometres from the centre of Liverpool. Originally private land, it became a country park just over a century ago.

From the bus stop on Upton Road, a path takes you through woods and across a footbridge high over a busy road, leading to the exposed sandstone ridge running along the top of the hill. Follow it and you will reach three interesting buildings, none of them now in use. The windmill, replacing an earlier mill destroyed by fire, dates from 1800 and was used to grind corn for flour for 75 years. Further on is the observatory, built in 1866. In 1929, it became part of the University of Liverpool Tidal Institute: the first tide-predicting machines in the world were created here, and up to the 1950s, the institute was responsible for predicting tides in two-thirds of the world. Beyond it is the lighthouse, built in 1873; visible for 22 kilometres, it warned ships of the sandbanks in the river mouth.

In the 18th century, the hill looked very different as it was covered with more than 100 flagpoles; when a merchant ship was spotted coming in, flags were hoisted as an alert, visible in the docks, so that stevedores would be ready to unload the boat as soon as it arrived. This money-saving signalling system was superseded by the telegraph, and now all that remains of it is a single hole in the sandstone, just north of the windmill.

Although the ridge is now fringed with trees, between the windmill and the observatory is a spot where the treetops are lower, providing superb views on either side. On the left extends the flat plane of the Wirral, with the sea and the North Wales coast beyond it. On the right you can see the docks on both sides of the Mersey, with the clustered towers of Liverpool appearing still and silent in the distance.

Address Bidston Hill, Wirral CH43 7PZ, www.bidstonhill.org.uk | **Getting there** Bus 437 from Sir Thomas Street to Bidston, Boundary Road or Noctorum Lane; or train to Bidston station, then 15-minute walk through Bidston Village. | **Hours** Windmill and lighthouse are occasionally open for tours, check website for details | **Tip** See the farm animals and visit the cafe at the delightful Tam O'Shanter Urban Farm, between Bidston Hill and Boundary Road (daily 9:30am–4:30pm).

16 Birkenhead Park

Crossing the Alps in Birkenhead

Hidden among the trees in Birkenhead Park is a spectacular re-creation of an Alpine rockery, the centrepiece of a mini European Grand Tour. The designer of Birkenhead Park – the world's first publicly funded park – was Joseph Paxton, head gardener at Chatsworth, the Devonshire family's opulent country estate in Derbyshire. There he had created a rock garden for the Duke of Devonshire as a reminder of the duke's visit to the Alps. Built on a hillside and incorporating a chasm and a waterfall, this wonder was widely admired, and the citizens of Birkenhead wanted one too.

Paxton used soil excavated for the creation of the park's lakes to form mounds, enabling him to make a steep slope as a setting for the rocks. He wanted visitors to come upon them unexpectedly, and placed the giant rocks in a secluded place surrounded by trees. At Chatsworth he had invented special machinery to position the rocks accurately, and his ability to cantilever them out from the hillside adds to the drama. The effect was intended to be part nature and part artifice, although he probably did not expect it to become a playground, a favoured place for hide-and-seek, as it now is for young visitors.

The remainder of the Grand Tour unfolds as you move through the park, like an architectural history lesson. Near the rocks are the charming Swiss Bridge and the Roman boathouse, while each of the perimeter lodges is dressed up in a different style – Norman, castellated, Gothic, and Italianate – with the Grand Entrance resembling a vast triumphal arch. After a visit to the grounds in 1850, Frederick Olmsted, founder of American landscape architecture, remarked, "I was ready to admit that in democratic America there was nothing to be thought of as comparable with this People's Garden." The fruits of his inspiration are seen in the great design for New York's Central Park.

Address Birkenhead Park, Park Street, Birkenhead CH41 4HY, Tel +44 1516525197 | **Getting there** 5-minute walk from Birkenhead Park station | **Tip** On the north side of the park is a modern visitor centre with an excellent cafe (daily 9am–4:30pm).

17 Birkenhead Priory

Worship and warships

Birkenhead Priory, founded in the mid-12th century, is the oldest building on Merseyside. Until its dissolution in 1536, it housed a small community of monks who controlled the ferry crossing to Liverpool. It remained a lonely ruin in the early 1800s, when the Scotsman William Laird bought land on the Cheshire side of the River Mersey and established a shipyard.

Laird was not only an industrialist, but also a man of vision whose ambition was to create a new metropolis that would avoid the social problems of overcrowding and squalor that he saw in Liverpool. His plan, which was designed by one of the architects of Edinburgh New Town, was extraordinarily ambitious, with grand squares and boulevards, all contained within a grid and linked to a complex of new docks.

The shipyard was built alongside the priory, which was adapted and enlarged to serve as the parish church. In the 1840s the grandiose town plan and the docks both faltered, but the shipyard went on to become the town's biggest industry. Beyond the churchyard wall, four graving docks were built with wharves and workshops spreading along the waterfront.

Laird pioneered the construction of iron ships and supplied warships for the Crimean War and the two World Wars. From this place more than 1,100 vessels were launched between 1829 and 1947, including the Cunard liner *Mauretania* and the aircraft carrier *Ark Royal*. Today the shipyard mostly refits rather than builds vessels, but the juxtaposition of ancient monastic ruins and huge ships makes an extraordinary sight. After inspecting the priory chapter house and undercroft, you can ascend the tower of the Victorian parish church for a bird's-eye view of the shipyards. The large tomb of the Laird family takes pride of place in the cloister below, but their real memorial is the thriving maritime industry that continues on the riverbank beyond.

Address Priory Street, Birkenhead CH41 5JH, Tel +44 1516524177, www.thebirkenheadpriory.org | **Getting there** 15-minute walk from Hamilton Square station or Woodside Ferry Terminal along the riverside promenade | **Hours** Summer, Wed–Fri 1pm–5pm, Sat–Sun 10am–5pm; winter, Wed–Fri noon–4pm, Sat–Sun 10am–4pm; admission free | **Tip** The finest view of the Liverpool waterfront is from Monk's Ferry, just north of Birkenhead Priory.

18 Black Pearl

Pirates at art

Built of driftwood on the shoreline at New Brighton by local artist Frank Lund (helped by his friend Major Mace and the ship's dog, Scooby), the *Black Pearl* has enjoyed a brief but eventful life of piracy.

The story began with the almost daily appearance of wondrous sea creatures along the sandbanks of the River Mersey in 2012. Dolphins and mermaids, sea dragons, and octopi were found basking in the sun, carved by Frank from flotsam and jetsam deposited by the waves. Frank is a retired accountant who abandoned his bean counting for whittling and beachcombing, heading down to the seashore each morning to see what the tide washed in.

One day, in January 2013, a much larger object was seen rising up from the sands: a pirate ship flying the Jolly Roger, with its scary picture of a skull and crossbones. It was not long before local children were scrambling aboard.

In May of that year, however, tragedy struck in the form of arsonists who set the ship alight, causing severe damage. The community rallied round and helped Frank and Major rebuild it, so that it had a very successful summer with many piratical events. Then came the December storms, and during an unusually high tide, the *Black Pearl* was observed sailing off into the Mersey, rats clinging to the mast as she went down. After salvage operations, the decking was replaced in time for Christmas and New Year celebrations, but the January storms also took their toll. Ever undaunted, the Pirates of New Brighton scoured the sands again, and with the aid of other buccaneers and the support of local companies, they rebuilt the ship on a yet more ambitious scale.

Since then it has braved both malicious attacks and the forces of nature to host many enjoyable pirate days. And even if it does succumb, in the words of one visitor, "as long as there are people and driftwood and spirit, it will always come back."

Address Tower Promenade, New Brighton, Wirral CH45 1NX, www.facebook.com/
TheBlackPearlNewBrighton | **Getting there** 15-minute walk along the esplanade from New
Brighton station; 30-minute walk along the esplanade from Seacombe ferry terminal | **Tip**
The Magazine Hotel (7 Magazine Brow), a 10-minute walk along the esplanade south of the
Black Pearl, is a traditional pub with a good selection of ales, a river view, and a beer garden.

19_Bling Bling Building

A palace for Herbert, the King of Bling

The hairdresser Herbert Howe is Liverpool's King of Bling, and his premises, opened in 2006, were designed by the celebrated architect Piers Gough to express his flamboyant personality. The five-storey building stands at the junction of the RopeWalks and Liverpool One. Its curved walls of green-tinted glass are punctured by three giant pods, which jut out in random fashion and are faced in gold-coloured metal sheeting, patinated to form a leopard print effect over time. Once inside, Liverpool's fashion elite are transported by glass lifts to five floors of salons finished in polished black marble, chrome, and mirrors. Herbert's salons promise head-turning cuts and unique hair colouring, as well as body and spa treatments to make clients feel beautiful inside and out.

The King of Bling, who began his hairdressing career 50 years ago, is a local celebrity. As well as setting trends in hair and beauty, he starred in the docusoap *Shampoo*, which can be viewed on YouTube; he is a regular on radio and TV shows, and features as pantomime Dame in local theatre. His Queenie's Christmas parties, named after his mother, and his star-studded gala balls, raise funds for children and families in need. Typical of his charity work is providing Christmas Day lunch at the Adelphi for hundreds of people without families or friends.

In April 2015, the eternally youthful Herbert was rushed to hospital after falling ill at the salon, and was subsequently operated on for a brain tumour. When he came round after the six-hour operation, his first words to the surgeon were, "Can you go out and get me a Bee Gees wig and teeth because when I come out of this I'll be singing 'Stayin' Alive.'" Three days later he was back "onstage" at his salon. It's not for nothing that he won a Scouseology Special Award for Services to Liverpool, as well as a Lifetime Achievement from the Fellowship of British Hairdressing.

Address 69 Hanover Street, Liverpool L1 3DY, Tel +44 1517097834, www.herbertofliverpool.co.uk | **Getting there** 3-minute walk from Central station | **Hours** Tue–Wed 10am–5pm, Thu 10am–8pm, Fri–Sat 9am–6pm, Sun and Mon closed | **Tip** Filter and Fox, a short walk away at 27 Duke Street, is open seven days a week from 8am until midnight, serving wine, coffee, cocktails, breakfast, sandwiches, and small plates in a friendly and informal ambience.

20 Bluecoat Display Centre

Contemporary craft shop and exhibition space

Tucked away at the back of the Bluecoat garden is a treasure house of desirable objects to admire and to buy. The Bluecoat Display Centre occupies a bright, airy space designed by local architect Maggie Pickles, with fittings by Liverpool designers Definitive. Even the sliding security shutter on the window is a custom design.

Founded in 1959 to promote contemporary craft and design, the centre was for many years devoted mainly to handmade pottery in the Bernard Leach tradition. You can still buy the work of John Leach and Richard Batterham here, but today the space reflects the more colourful and experimental craft scene that has blossomed in recent decades. The display in the shop window on College Lane by the featured artist of the month could be gigantic wire sculptures of birds, cut-paper garlands, pleated scarves, or crazy machines made of recycled food tins.

Director Maureen Bampton, who has run the centre with great flair since 1986, likes to keep a balance between big names, such as jeweller Wendy Ramshaw or textile artist Michael Brennand-Wood, and lesser-known mid-career artists, but also has an eye for emerging talent. There are six exhibitions a year, which are always worth seeing, but for most visitors the main attraction is the shop. It stocks work by more than 60 local and 300 national and international craftspeople and artists.

The Bluecoat Display Centre is a charity; profits from the shop support the educational programme, which includes professional development sessions, opportunities for work experience for students, and advice on how to commission that one-off piece you have always dreamed of owning. You can spend anything from a few pounds on a pretty card to a few thousand on a museum-quality work; and by courtesy of Arts Council England's Own Art scheme, you can pay by interest-free instalments.

Address College Lane, Liverpool L 1 3BZ, Tel +44 1517094014, www.bluecoatdisplaycentre.com | **Getting there** 5-minute walk from Central station or Liverpool One bus station | **Hours** Mon – Sat 10am – 5:30pm, Sun noon – 5pm | **Tip** Recover from your shopping expedition with a glass of champagne at the glitzy Wow Bar in the Harvey Nichols Beauty Bazaar, around the corner at 16 Manesty's Lane.

21 The Bluecoat Garden

Yoko Ono is waiting for your wish

Where better to sit and dream than the Bluecoat garden, a tranquil haven only minutes away from the hubbub of the shopping streets. The handsome 18th-century building began life as a charity school, but in 1907, a group of artists set up studios here and 20 years later they established the Bluecoat Society for the Arts, Britain's oldest art centre. When a version of Roger Fry's controversial First Impressionist Exhibition was shown here in 1911, it was the first time paintings by Picasso, Matisse, Cezanne, and Van Gogh had been seen in Liverpool. Pavlova gave a talk about ballet; Stravinsky was entertained at lunch; Augustus John exhibited; George Melly came to fancy-dress parties as a boy; the young Simon Rattle attended music classes; Doris Lessing gave readings; Michael Clark danced – there is always something extraordinary going on.

The garden, a modest left-over space behind the main block, has been transformed with trees, shrubs, and seating into a great place for people-watching, coffee, or a lunchtime snack. Art events often spill out from the galleries: sculptured creatures hang in the trees and musicians strum.

Yoko Ono performed here twice, in 1967 and in 2008, when she had a tree placed in the garden, inviting visitors to write a wish and tie it on to the branches. Yoko has had the wishes from Liverpool and her other exhibitions buried at the foot of the Imagine Peace Tower, a column of light reaching into the sky on an island near Reykjavik. So far she has received more than a million wishes from her fans. The tower, powered by geothermal energy, is dedicated to John Lennon's dream of world peace, and is lit up at night on the anniversaries of his birth and death, on Yoko's birthday, and at the spring and winter equinoxes. Although her wish tree is no longer at the Bluecoat, you can still send Yoko your wish on the website, www.imaginepeacetower.com.

Address School Lane, Liverpool L 1 3BX, Tel +44 1517025324, www.thebluecoat.org.uk | **Getting there** 5-minute walk from Central station or Liverpool One bus station | **Hours** Mon–Sat 9am–6pm, Sun 11am–6pm | **Tip** Just outside the front gates is the legendary vinyl shop Probe Records, with a huge selection of punk, post-punk, indie, funk, soul, reggae, dub, electro, garage, krautrock, and freakbeat.

22 The Brink

Shampagne cocktail anyone?

If you want a truly original drinking experience, you will find it in a tin shed in the RopeWalks area. But don't expect to see any booze here, for the Brink is non-alcoholic. A social enterprise started by the charity Action on Addiction in 2011, it pioneered the modern dry bar, which is now catching on in other cities.

The Brink was set up because Liverpool has one of the highest rates of alcoholism in England; but the organisers wanted the place to work for everybody, not just people in recovery. And it does. The ambience in the Brink is laid-back and not a bit institutional. The eclectic interior seems to have been designed to look as though it has not been designed: scaffolding is combined with plush armchairs and oversized wooden tables, although the upside-down houseplants are a touch outré.

Staff and customers may include former drinkers but the place has rapidly caught on with a wider public who are fed up with the boring selection of non-alcoholic beverages on sale in pubs and bars. Among the huge range of drinks on offer besides the obvious teas, coffees, and mineral waters are smoothies; fruit and vegetable presses made to order; unusual virgin cocktails involving flavours of a vanished era, such as Mawson's sarsaparilla, and dandelion and burdock; and cordials by Mister Fitzpatricks, whose temperance bar in Rawtenstall is the last one in the country to survive. The unpretentious but delicious food includes breakfast, soups, sandwiches, mezze, fish and chips, and afternoon tea.

Something else to enjoy here: the puns. The cocktail menu features such wittily named libations as Nojitos and Brink Panthers; there are humorous slogans on the skylights and poems on the walls; and among the numerous activities – music gigs, art classes, film nights, family Sunday roasts – is the Raucous Caucus Recovery Chorus, which rehearses here every Tuesday night.

Address 15–21 Parr Street, Liverpool L 1 4JN, Tel +44 1517030582, www.thebrinkliverpool.com | **Getting there** 10-minute walk from Central station | **Hours** Mon–Fri 9am–11pm, Sat 10am–11pm, Sun 11am–10pm | **Tip** Coldplay, Barry Manilow, Badly Drawn Boy, and Take That are among the many famous artists who have made recordings at nearby Parr Street Studios, a Grammy Award-winning studio complex incorporating a hotel and two bars.

23 Bucket Fountain

A 1960s kinetic sound sculpture with water

As you walk into Beetham Plaza, a traffic-free space tucked between office and apartment blocks, your ears are assailed by the roaring and crashing sounds of water. The noise comes from the Bucket Fountain, installed in 1967. It has 20 "buckets" which fill up and abruptly tip over, releasing their contents into the pool below; as each vessel empties it rights itself for refilling. The staircases leading up to two viewing platforms overlooking the fountain conceal the water pumps and an air vent for the car park below the piazza. The space-age curves of the fountain's stainless-steel containers are typical of sixties-era design.

Welsh designer Richard Huws, a lecturer at the University of Liverpool, was determined to reinvent the fountain for the 20th century. For the 1951 Festival of Britain he created the 13-metre-high Water Mobile, also involving hinged containers of water tipping over. It was, in his words, "a breakthrough in fountain design," but it kept going wrong. By the time Merseyside Civic Society asked him for a fountain in Liverpool, he had refined the design and worked out how to keep the water flowing smoothly while the cups filled and emptied at random.

The fountain was fabricated for him at Cammell Laird's Birkenhead shipyard; he had served as an apprentice there before studying naval architecture at the University of Liverpool and sculpture at art school in Vienna. He also worked on the design of the Spitfire fighter aircraft made famous during World War II. This unusual education convinced him of the need to break down the barriers between art, architecture, and engineering. In his fountain, the result was, as he put it, "a waterfall of a strange new kind. Instead of streaming steadily, water hurtles down unexpectedly in detached lumps in all directions." The hypnotic combination of sound and movement has fascinated Merseysiders ever since.

Address Beetham Plaza, Liverpool L 2 0XJ | **Getting there** 3-minute walk from James Street station | **Tip** Nearby, on the corner of Brunswick and Lower Castle streets, Caffè Nero, formerly the Adelphi Bank, has beautiful bronze doors with scenes of brotherly love including Castor and Pollux, and David and Jonathan.

24 __ Burne-Jones Windows

A Pre-Raphaelite vision of paradise

The interior of All Hallows Church is a glorious picture gallery of stained glass. Fourteen of its fifteen windows were designed by Edward Burne-Jones, Pre-Raphaelite painter and principal stained-glass designer for Morris and Co, the famous design firm founded by his friend William Morris. Their windows transformed Victorian churches with radiant colour harmonies, flowing lines, and captivating details such as music-making angels or patterns of leaves and flowers.

The nave windows, glowing with unusually deep shades of rose, pink, mauve, and dark blue, tell the story of Christ: his early life from birth to baptism on the north side, and later events including the Crucifixion and Resurrection on the south. The designs date from the 1880s and their elongated figures and simplified curves are typical of the later work of Burne-Jones. The figures in his earlier work are fuller and more rounded, as in the great west window (1875 – 76) depicting the four evangelists, Matthew, Mark, Luke, and John, each with a small Biblical scene below; the delightful panels depicting flowers against rich green backgrounds were designed by Morris. Also of this date is the east window, "The Adoration of the Holy Lamb," with the rivers of paradise flowing down from the lamb, the symbols of the evangelists, and a host of angels.

This holy magnificence is a product of the mercantile wealth of Victorian Liverpool: nowhere else will you see such an outstanding group of Burne-Jones windows. The church was built at the expense of John Bibby, whose father founded the Bibby shipping line. The church was a tribute to Bibby's wife, Fanny, the daughter of Jesse Hartley, architect of the Albert Dock. She is also commemorated in a white marble statue by the Italian sculptor Frederigo Fabiani, showing her soul floating up to heaven, enveloped in undulating marble draperies and accompanied by an angel.

Address All Hallows Church, corner of Greenhill and Allerton roads, Allerton, Liverpool L18 6JJ, Tel +44 1517246391, www.allhallowsallerton.org.uk | **Getting there** Bus 86 or 86A from Liverpool One bus station to Allerton, Ballantrae Road, then a 5-minute walk | **Hours** Apr–Oct, Tue 2pm–4pm | **Tip** Three of Burne-Jones's most famous paintings can be seen at the Lady Lever Art Gallery, Port Sunlight (see p. 188).

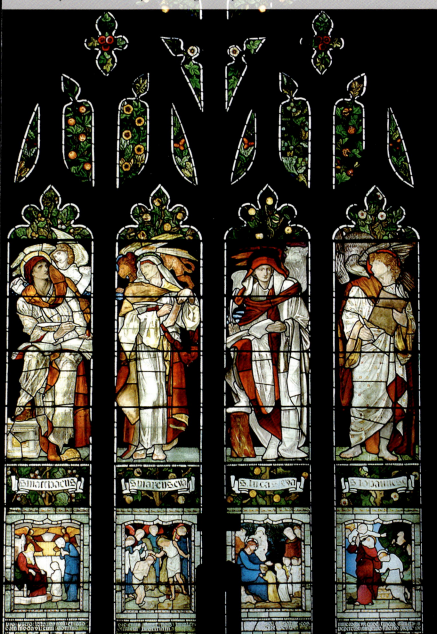

25 __ The Calderstones

Megalithic rock art in a parkland setting

In Calderstones Park there stand six mysterious sandstone blocks carved with sacred symbols. Dating from the late Neolithic period or early Bronze Age, they were once part of a megalithic tomb within the locality. The stones probably formed a roofed passage leading to the burial chamber, as found in two surviving tombs in Anglesey of a similar date, and are carved with curious spirals, concentric circles, cup marks, and footprints. The footprint carvings in particular are very unusual, the closest parallel being with a tomb in Brittany. The exact meaning of the rock engravings is not known, but they can be assumed to be religious symbols related to burial. It is possible that the marks formed part of a visual language comprehensible only to an elite and the dead, for the Anglesey sites show that the art could not be read except from within the burial chamber.

It was only in the mid-19th century, when the building of large houses began in the area, that interest in the origins of the Calderstones developed. In 1845, some years after the tumulus had been levelled, Joseph Walker, for whom Calderstones Mansion House was erected, had the surviving stones gathered together and set up in a circle at the entrance to his estate. In 1902, the estate was acquired by Liverpool Corporation, which opened it as a public park, and later placed the stones under cover in a glass house within the grounds.

In recent years there has been public concern about their deterioration, and plans are now in place to move them again. This is being promoted by the Reader Organisation, a charity that is currently renovating the house and stables as an International Centre for Reading and Wellbeing, taking advantage of the beautiful parkland setting. An important part of this imaginative project is to create a permanent and dignified home for the ancient and sacred stones after which the park is named.

Address Calderstones Park, Liverpool L18 3JB, Tel +44 1517292200, www.thereader.org.uk | **Getting there** Bus 75 or 76 from Liverpool One bus station to Allerton, Green Lane, then a 5-minute walk | **Hours** Park open 24/7; for access to the Calderstones, contact the Reader Organisation, details above | **Tip** Within the flower garden of Calderstones Park is a monument to Jet of Iada, a German shepherd dog which saved the lives of many people trapped underground by the blitz during World War II. Jet received the Dickin Medal, the animals VC, for outstanding gallantry and devotion to duty.

26__ Camp and Furnace

Post-industrial party venue

Until recently, Camp and Furnace was a collection of leaky industrial buildings used as a foundry, a blade factory, a coachbuilder's, and latterly, a scrapyard, before being restored as an art space for the Liverpool Biennial. Then it was taken over by an architect, a designer, a couple of musicians, and a chef. They turned it into a unique venue, using its raw industrial aesthetic as a backdrop for eating, drinking, clubbing, pop-up events, and just bringing people together.

There are two main spaces. Camp is used for live music, film, and sports events on a giant screen. A photomural of massed tree trunks, a collection of vintage caravans, and twinkling fairy lights provide a quirky outdoorsy feel. Furnace is vast; you gasp at its size (9,000 square feet), its cavernous roof, with steel girders and gantries still in place, and the smoke-stained brick furnace at the far end. Linking the two spaces is the Lobby Bar, lit by naked bulbs, with a bar made of unfinished wood and a long communal table. In winter, a log fire blazes in a wood-burning stove. And that's just the public side: there are also photography studios and spaces used to film pop videos, television dramas, and feature films.

The Lobby Bar serves an interesting menu of small and large plates in a laid-back atmosphere. On Friday and Saturday nights the tempo increases for the Food Slams, when Furnace becomes a combination of nightclub and street-food market, with food stalls, bartenders shaking cocktails, and disco music. The food changes for each Slam, bringing in new trends and tastes. On Sunday the stalls disappear, the atmosphere relaxes for brunch, and after that, hearty Sunday roasts are served at long trestle tables. Special events include Bingo (but not as you know it) and Laces Out!, a festival for trainer and sneaker freaks. Everyone loves the place – cool youngsters, ageing hippies, families; they come not just for the food, the drink, or the music, but also for the experience.

Address 67 Greenland Street, Liverpool L 1 0BY, Tel +44 1517082890, www.campandfurnace.com | **Getting there** 20-minute walk from Central station; bus 82A from Liverpool One bus station to Stanhope Street | **Hours** Mon–Tue 10am–6pm, Wed 10am–11pm, Thu 10am–1am, Fri–Sat 10am–2:30am, Sun 10am–10pm; food served Mon–Fri noon–5pm, Sat 3pm–midnight, Sun noon–6pm | **Tip** Across Parliament Street is the splendid Cain's Brewery building, decorated with Cain's gazelle symbol in terracotta. There are plans to create a brewery village with apartments and a boutique hotel.

27___Canning Street
The Georgian Quarter

This impressive street of splendid terraced houses is the heart of what is known as the Georgian Quarter, although most of the area dates from shortly after the death of George IV, in 1830. Little known beyond the north-west of England, the Georgian Quarter is one of the best-preserved examples of historic urban architecture outside London. Canning Street is named after British statesman George Canning, who has the distinction of being the shortest-serving prime minister: he died in office in August 1827, just 119 days after his appointment.

The quarter was laid out from 1827 according to a plan by the corporation surveyor John Foster Sr. Designed to link up with the town centre, it consists of a grid of streets flanked by grand parades of three-storey homes with basements. Restrictive covenants precluded lower-class housing, and specified the style and materials to be used. Canning Street, the quarter's longest, displays all the decorative features that give the area its refined character. These include iron railings at street level, projecting porches with Ionic columns, iron balconies, and tall sash windows. At the end of Canning Street is Falkner Square, with white stuccoed houses around a leafy garden. Percy Street, which leads off Canning Street near the cathedral, differs from the rest of the area, its stone-faced buildings reminiscent of Edinburgh.

After World War I, the Georgian Quarter went into decline, the wealthy occupants deserting it for the suburbs, and parts of it were demolished by the University of Liverpool. By the 1960s, it had become the red light district, its neglected houses converted to bedsits. Fortunately the city council held the freeholds and was able to repossess the worst properties and hand them over to social landlords. Gradually the houses were restored, and today it is one of the most sought-after places in the city to live.

Address Canning Street, Liverpool L8 7NN | **Getting there** Bus 82, 86, or CityLink from Liverpool One bus station; 15-minute walk from Central station | **Tip** St Philip Neri, the University of Liverpool Catholic Chaplaincy, has a Byzantine-style interior with splendid mosaics, and an Italian garden (30 Catharine Street, www.cathchap.org.uk).

28__Casbah Coffee Club

Where the Beatles played before they were the Beatles

Superficially, the Casbah is nothing much, just a few small low-ceilinged rooms lined in dark wood and black-painted brick in the cellar of a Victorian villa. The house, in a leafy suburban street, had previously been the local Conservative Club. It seems an unlikely setting for the birth of the music that rocked the world.

Mona Best, mother of the drummer Pete Best, founded the club in the basement of her home as a place for her teenage sons to hang out and make music with their friends: now Pete's brothers take tour groups around the club and share their memories, laced with inimitable Scouse wit. They describe how John Lennon, Paul McCartney, and George Harrison, then playing in a group called the Quarrymen, helped get the club ready and played on the opening night, August 29, 1959. You can still see the ceilings they painted, John's in silver with Aztec-style motifs, and Paul's with rainbow stripes. When the club was enlarged, Pete painted a spider's web behind the new stage area. Near the bar where instant coffee and Coca-Cola was served, John's girlfriend Cynthia painted his silhouette in silver, a reference to the Silver Beatles, the name later taken by the group before becoming simply the Beatles.

In those early days, John, Paul, George, and their friends regarded the Casbah as their personal hangout; they ate, drank, slept, and played there, encouraged and fed by Mona. Pete played drums in the Blackjacks, the club's resident group; Cilla Black and Gerry and the Pacemakers played there. The club had over 1,000 members: when crowded with sweaty bodies, it must have been like the Black Hole of Calcutta. When the Beatles went to Hamburg in 1960, Pete joined them as drummer, but in 1962, after they came back, he got the sack, and soon after, Mona closed the club. Hardly changed since then, it breathes the authentic atmosphere of the early days of Merseybeat.

Address 8 Hayman's Green West Derby, Liverpool L12 7JG, Tel +44 7872017473, www.petebest.com/casbah-coffee-club.aspx | **Getting there** Bus 12 or 13 from Queen Square bus station to Mill Lane, West Derby | **Hours** Daily 10am–5pm; tour booking essential | **Tip** In West Derby village centre, the Elizabethan Court House (open Sundays from 2pm to 4pm, April to October), preserves its 17th- and 18th-century fittings, and nearby are the gates to Croxteth Country Park.

29 __ Chambré Hardman's Kitchen

For fans of fifties kitchenalia

When the National Trust took over No. 59 Rodney Street, they found that hardly anything had ever been thrown away. The house had latterly been the studio and home of the portrait photographer Edward Chambré Hardman and his wife, Margaret. He lived and worked here for 40 years, until his death, in 1988.

This makes it unique in the history of photography, as there is no other example in Britain of a photographic studio that survives with all its paraphernalia – lights, cameras, darkroom equipment, mounting card, and retouching inks, as well as studio records, prints, and negatives. While most visitors will come to find out about Hardman the photographer, the house is also a gold mine for domestic historians.

The kitchen is one of the most evocative rooms in the house. The couple moved in soon after the war, when rationing was still in force. This was long before the days of fitted kitchens: there is a frugal make-do-and-mend feeling about the tiny room, decorated in cream and pale green. Mismatched cupboards, tables, cabinets, and shelves jostle for space. There are ancient food packets and tins – Heinz spaghetti, Rowntree's cocoa, and Tate and Lyle sugar, and some long-forgotten brands: Kardomah tea, Caledonia oatcakes, Patriot Brand coffee essence, and Barker and Dobson chocolate éclairs. Every surface, from the tops of the cabinets to the draining board, is crowded with bottles, jars, and cheap-looking pans and kettles. There is a bread bin, a kitchen scale, old newspapers, and bottles of plonk.

The Hardmans cannot have been very domestic as the only oven is a Baby Belling, with a two-ring electric hob next to it. There is also a Goblin vacuum cleaner, but, as Margaret is reputed to have said, "What do Scotland and our kitchen have in common? Both have islands of Muck."

Address 59 Rodney Street, Liverpool L1 9ER (ticket office in Pilgrim Street, behind the house), Tel +44 1517096261, www.nationaltrust.org.uk/hardmans-house | **Getting there** 15-minute walk from Central station; CityLink bus from Liverpool One bus station to Upper Duke Street | **Hours** Late Mar–Oct, Wed–Sat 11am–3:30pm | **Tip** The Pilgrim (34 Pilgrim Street) is a lively pub popular with students and locals for its real ale and excellent inexpensive food.

30__ Chavasse Park

The place to let your credit card cool down

Chavasse Park is a rare thing: a totally modern city-centre park. Its five acres of beautifully landscaped gardens opened in 2008 as an integral part of the new Liverpool One shopping development. The park is named after members of the local Chavasse family: Francis, who was the second bishop of Liverpool from 1900 to 1923, and his twin sons, Christopher and Noel, who were both Olympic athletes. Noel is also one of only three men to have won the Victoria Cross twice, and his memorial can be seen in one of the landscaped borders. The area now occupied by the park was totally destroyed in the blitz of 1941 and left undeveloped for more than 60 years.

The park was one of the last phases of Liverpool One to be completed: it sits on top of service roads leading to the shops and a four-level underground car park. The site is oval in shape and is sheltered on the north side by One Park West, a tall apartment block with a corner like the prow of a ship, designed by César Pelli, architect of the Petronas Towers in Kuala Lumpur. Out of concern for the environment, Chavasse Park is built to retain rainwater for irrigation in special water-harvesting tanks.

At the park's summit, fringed by bars and restaurants, is the Grand Lawn, a grassy area for picnicking and events, including live music, theatre performances, and family activities. From here a series of colourfully planted terraces and pathways descend to the Strand, leading on to the Albert Dock and the waterfront. There are avenues of mature trees, and gardens with herbaceous borders, shrubs, and grasses, while climbers such as wisteria and clematis clothe the perimeter stone walls. Secluded benches are much in demand for courting couples. At street level are fountains and water gardens that mark the former entrance to the Old Dock (see p. 154). The park is a peaceful spot and makes a great place to chill out after all that stressful shopping.

Address Chavasse Park, Liverpool One, Liverpool L 1 8LT, www.liverpoolone.com/chavasse_park.aspx | **Getting there** 2-minute walk from Liverpool One bus station; 5-minute walk from James Street station | **Hours** 24/7 | **Tip** Tavern on the Green (9 Kenyon Steps), specialising in cool lagers and cocktails, is a favoured bar overlooking the park.

31__ Christopher Columbus Statue

The discoverer of America was the maker of Liverpool

This startling claim is written below the statue of Christopher Columbus outside the Palm House in Sefton Park. The spectacular conservatory with three tiers of curved glass roofs is a popular venue for weddings and parties; especially when lit up at night, the crystalline vision of iron and glass is a magical sight. Most days, it is open to all to stroll under the palms, or to enjoy the yoga or salsa sessions held there. What would its founder have thought?

Henry Yates Thomson, who gave the Palm House to the people of Liverpool, was the millionaire son of a local banker. Typical of his class, he felt that his gift to the populace had to come with a dose of instruction. He had eight statues made for the Palm House. Four were of horticulturalists: John Parkinson, botanical writer and apothecary to James I; André Le Nôtre, designer of the park at Versailles; Carl Linnaeus, Swedish botanist and founder of plant classification; and Charles Darwin, author of *On The Origin of Species*. The other four were involved in exploration: Henry the Navigator, sponsor of Portuguese voyages of discovery; Gerardus Mercator, mapmaker; Captain Cook, explorer; and Columbus.

The assertion that Columbus's discovery of America was the making of Liverpool was intended as a history lesson for park visitors. Behind it lay pride in Liverpool's position as an international mercantile city, which was at its height when the Palm House first opened in 1896. Today, we are not so proud of this legacy: initially the city's wealth came from the infamous triangular trade, whereby Liverpool merchant ships took manufactured goods to Africa to be traded for slaves; the ships then brought the slaves to America and sold them for goods produced with slave labour – tobacco, sugar, coffee, and later, cotton.

Address Sefton Park, Liverpool L17 1AP (for Sat Nav use L17 1AL), Tel +44 1517262415, www.palmhouse.org.uk | **Getting there** 20-minute walk from St Michael's station; buses from Liverpool One bus station: 75 or 80 to Sefton Park, Hartington Road, then a 15-minute walk; 82 to Dingle, Allington Street, then a 15-minute walk | **Hours** Apr–Oct, daily 10:30am–6:30pm, Nov–Feb, daily 10:30am–4pm; sometimes closes early for special events, check website | **Tip** In the woods behind the Palm House is a bird-feeding station where spoonbills and ringneck parakeets have been spotted.

32__Cow & Co Cafe
Coffee, waffles, music, magazines, and design

Cow & Co began life in 2009 as a design store selling a carefully edited selection of beautiful objects – lighting, furniture, tableware, stationery – all with a clean, graphic look. Founders Nicola and Benji Holroyd started to serve coffee as an added service to their customers; gradually the food-and-drink side expanded and Cow & Co turned into a cafe that also sold good design. Now the gifts and objects have taken a back seat, although they are available in an online shop; but Cow & Co is still a place where aesthetics inform every aspect of the operation, making it a pleasure to visit.

Located in a tiny converted Victorian shop, Cow and Co has tables outside on the pavement for the summer and a cosy atmosphere inside during the winter. Everything has been carefully designed with attention to detail: natural pale wood surfaces contrast with the deep blue colour of the panels behind the bar, which is relieved by simple white typography listing the artisan coffee drinks and loose-leaf teas. These are served in beautiful hand-thrown pottery cups and saucers, which you can buy online.

Cow & Co is not just concerned with the way things look: taste is also a priority. Top-quality environmentally sourced, sustainable coffee comes from Origin, an ethical coffee importer. The seasonally changing breakfast and lunch menus include artisan bread, toast, interesting sandwiches, soup, bagels, and waffles. Tea is provided by Leaf, and the cakes come in unusual flavours, such as apple and caramel, or lime and courgette with pistachio. The menu also features a range of wines and Liverpool craft beers.

Two more features single out Cow & Co from other coffee shops: the cool soundtrack, with playlists published on their website, and a huge range of stylish design and lifestyle magazines – such as *Monocle*, *Apartamento*, *Mousse*, *Cherry Bombe*, and *Kinfolk* – available to read and to buy.

Address 15 Cleveland Square, Liverpool L1 5BE, Tel +44 1517091516, www.cowandcocafe.com | **Getting there** 10-minute walk from Central station | **Hours** Mon–Fri 9am–6pm, Sat 10am–6pm, Sun 10am–4pm | **Tip** At the corner of Park Street is a memorial garden on the site of the demolished St Thomas's Church, where Joseph Williamson, founder of the Tunnels (see p. 226), was buried.

33__Cricket

Where the wives and girlfriends shop

Cricket is Liverpool's high-fashion super-boutique, a clothes shop like no other. Don't expect to find a few precious garments tastefully presented under a spotlight, or the bag du jour isolated on a marble shelf as if it were in a museum. Cricket is as crowded and colourful as a sweet shop, and visiting it is a visual feast. There are bags massed on shelves, walls of shoes, and rails crammed with clothes, but nothing bland or beige. You will see adventurous deconstructed pieces, fabulously wild prints, lacy little numbers, bold knits, and glitzy trainers, by labels such as Balenciaga, Kenzo, Céline, Givenchy, Stella McCartney, Matthew Williamson, and Christian Louboutin. There are no snooty assistants whose looks say, "You can't afford it." Cricket is friendly. The staff will be happy to talk you through the latest arrivals, or you can look around on your own; and you don't have to buy.

Justine Mills started Cricket in 1991 to sell men's clothes – which she still does – but after a few years, her all-consuming enthusiasm for women's fashion took over. Every February and September she attends the fashion weeks in Paris, Milan, New York, and London. Her buying power is respected; she gets front-row seats at many of the shows; she places her orders and brings avant-garde catwalk looks straight to Merseyside. Liverpool girls are adventurous, so Mills sees no point in selling middle-of-the-road clothes that are available at other shops; she knows her customers – they want to look like what they see in the magazines and at the awards ceremonies.

Cricket hit the headlines when Colleen Rooney bought her wedding outfit here, but its success shows it is not just a shop for footballers' wives: among its best customers are Chinese students at Liverpool University returning home, taking with them those special pieces they can't get anywhere else.

Address 9 Cavern Walks, Matthew Street, Liverpool L 2 6RE, Tel +44 1512274645, www.cricket-fashion.com | **Getting there** 5-minute walk from James Street station | **Hours** Mon–Sat 9:30am–5:30pm, Sun noon–4pm | **Tip** Sink into a sofa and recover from shopping with tea and homemade cakes at Rococo (61 Lord Street, first floor, www.rococoliverpool.com).

34_ Crowne Plaza Liverpool – John Lennon Airport

Liverpool in the golden age of flying

Today Liverpool is served by the modern John Lennon Airport; but two miles closer to the city is the original 1930s terminal building which has been imaginatively converted into a hotel. With the advent of air travel after World War I, the great seaport of Liverpool was determined to remain the leading Atlantic hub. As well as docks, an airport was needed and the ancient Speke Manor on the bank of the River Mersey was acquired to create just such an "air-junction." Flights began in 1930, served by converted farmsteads and barns until the terminal building and two massive hangars were opened.

The terminal building is at the centre, with three decks that originally served as viewing platforms. From the tall tower a neon signal flashed out, in Morse code, the letters LV for Liverpool. During World War II, Royal Air Force fighter squadrons stationed at Speke played a major role in protecting the approaches to the Port of Liverpool. After the war, Manchester overtook Liverpool as an international airport until the age of budget airlines, when the city decided to invest in a new facility concentrating on European travellers. At first the old terminal and hangars were abandoned, but it was soon recognised that their advanced engineering, suave Art Deco styling, and excellent state of preservation put them on par with the airports at Paris Le Bourget and Berlin Templehof as leading examples of European aviation history; and in time the old Liverpool structures were saved. The terminal building became a 4-star hotel, bar, and restaurant, disregarding the usual corporate look for an aeronautical theme, while one of the hangars is a gym. On the forecourt, where passengers used to embark, local enthusiasts are restoring a fine collection of vintage aircraft, which recalls the golden age of flying.

Address Speke Road, Liverpool L 24 8QD, Tel +44 1514945000, www.crowne-plaza-liverpool.co.uk | **Getting there** Bus 27, 82, or 86A from Liverpool One bus station to Ravenside Retail Park, Speke Road | **Tip** Just beyond the new airport is Speke Hall, a historic half-timbered Tudor house owned by the National Trust. Buses to the Liverpool airport stop at the Walk, a 20-minute stroll to the hall.

35 Dafna's Cheesecake Factory

Like Grandmother used to bake

This modest shop at a busy road junction not far from Penny Lane is one of a kind that has almost disappeared from our high streets: the homemade cake shop. No fancy French patisserie here, no overcomplicated showpieces – just good old-fashioned cakes.

Dafna's Cheesecake Factory was started by Anne Lev after a visit to Chicago, where she tasted "the most wonderful cheesecake in the world." Anne brought the recipe back to Liverpool and served it at her son's bar mitzvah, where it was such a hit that all her friends kept asking for more. She started making cheesecake at home for local restaurants and delicatessens and then opened the shop in Smithdown Road in 1977 in an old dairy, continuing to supply discerning cafes and restaurants, and extending her range of offerings. She now offers cheesecake in nine tempting flavours, as well as carrot cake, coffee and walnut cake, chocolate fudge cake, Guinness cake, lemon drizzle cake, ginger-and-cinnamon cake, polenta cake, brownies, shortbreads, gluten-free and vegan cakes, and a selection of desserts such as chocolate roulade and pear frangipane.

All her cakes are made using time-honoured recipes and high-quality ingredients. Anne employs a few home bakers, but most of the confections are prepared in the on-site kitchen, filling the shop with glorious aromas. She still takes pride in working behind the counter, and enjoys talking to her customers: many of her original fans were students who now bring in their children. She even gets a name-check in one of Frank Cottrell Boyce's children's books.

Prices are amazingly reasonable: Anne has never sought to make huge amounts of money and you can buy a single slice or a whole cake. And who was Dafna? Not a person, but the name of a boat owned by Anne and her husband Yacov, a sea captain.

Address 240 Smithdown Road Liverpool L15 5AH, Tel +44 1517337808, www.dafna.co.uk | **Getting there** Bus 75, 76, 80, or 80A from Liverpool One bus station to Lathbury Lane | **Hours** Mon–Sat 9am–5:30pm | **Tip** Round the corner is Richard Behrend's music shop (8 Greenbank Road), selling brass, woodwind, and stringed instruments; sheet music, and musical gifts.

36 Dazzle Ferry

See the city from the river

It is exhilarating to cross the Mersey by ferry on a fine day: if you are going to work, the morning trip sets you up for the day and the return journey clears the mind. Today most commuters cross the Mersey by going underneath it by car, bus, or train; the days are gone when thousands of bowler-hatted businessmen walked round and round on deck for their morning constitutional.

A great way to enjoy the ferry is by taking a River Explorer Cruise, starting at the Pier Head, crossing to Seacombe, then going up-river to Birkenhead Woodside, and back to Liverpool. As the ferry pulls away from the Pier Head to the strains of Gerry and the Pacemakers, the Three Graces look their magnificent best. Soon the clustered skyscrapers of the new Liverpool and the vast area of the north docks, once bustling with activity, come into view. Beyond the wind turbines and the mountains of scrap metal waiting to be shipped to China is the new Liverpool2 deepwater container port, able to handle mega-size container vessels. On both sides of the river are tunnel ventilation towers styled like 1960s hi-fi sets. After Woodside, the ferry passes the massive Cammell Laird ship-repairing sheds before crossing back to Liverpool.

A bonus for ferry riders is the eye-popping Dazzle Ferry, timed to coincide with the First World War centenary commemorations. One of the ferries, the *Snowdrop*, has been repainted by veteran Pop artist Peter Blake, with brilliantly coloured stripes, targets, and zigzags in homage to the 4,000 merchant navy vessels and 400 warships painted with camouflage patterns to make them difficult to spot. An onboard exhibition tells the story of the dazzle ships, many of which were painted in the Liverpool docks. The *Snowdrop* will eventually return to its normal livery, but whatever the colour, a "Ferry Cross the Mersey" will always be the quintessential Liverpool experience.

Address Mersey Ferries Terminal, Pier Head, George's Parade, Liverpool L 3 1DP, Tel +44 1513301444 | **Getting there** 5-minute walk from James Street station; 10-minute walk from Liverpool One bus station | **Hours** Apr–Oct, River Explorer Cruise departs Pier Head on the hour Mon–Fri 10am–4pm, Sat–Sun 10am–6pm, duration 50 minutes | **Tip** Free guided tours of the pilot ship *Edmund Gardner*, kept in dry dock near the Museum of Liverpool, are held in the summer; booking is essential (Tel +44 1514784499).

37 __Delifonseca Dockside

Shop and eat in a foodie's Aladdin's cave

Delifonseca is named after its founder, Candice Fonseca, a self-confessed "mad foodie," born to a Portuguese family in Hong Kong and raised in Bury, both famous for their markets. In 2006, frustrated by the lack of speciality food shops in Liverpool, she threw in her career in the film industry and started the first Delifonseca, in Stanley Street.

Four years later, she took another gamble and moved into much larger premises, formerly a Harry Ramsden's fish-and-chips restaurant about one mile outside the city centre. Although the tarmac surroundings are unpromising, there is plenty of parking space, and once you are inside, Delifonseca Dockside certainly has the wow factor. It's huge, and packed with everything for the foodie, mad or otherwise. Whether you are looking for high-quality store-cupboard basics, the latest ingredient recommended by your favourite celebrity chef, an unusual gift, or something to nibble right now, you will find it here.

There are foodstuffs from all over the world, many from small artisan producers, all beautifully packaged and temptingly displayed – oils, pastas, rice, flours, olives, biscuits, chocolates, preserves, relishes, spices, sauces, condiments, vinegars, teas, coffees, wines, spirits, cordials, and crackers. There are also fresh foods in abundance – cheeses, charcuterie, meat from Brough's local butchery, breads from the German bakery, and an array of fruit and vegetables.

Next to the shop is a restaurant, serving a changing menu based on seasonal and local produce, headed by famous local chef Martin Cooper, who offers his unfussy modern take on traditional dishes. Meanwhile the original deli in Stanley Street is now Fonseca's, a wine bar and restaurant with a mini-deli counter for take-out gourmet sandwiches. No wonder Delifonseca is a now a regular in good food awards and restaurant guides.

Address Brunswick Dock, Liverpool L 3 4BN (Sat Nav L 8 6PZ), Tel +44 1512550808, www.delifonseca.co.uk | **Getting there** 5-minute walk from Brunswick station; bus 82A or C5 from Liverpool One bus station to Brunswick Dock | **Hours** Deli: Mon–Sat 8am–9pm, Sun 9:30am–5pm; Restaurant: Mon–Thu 8am–9pm, Fri–Sat 8am–9:30pm, Sun 9:30am–5pm | **Tip** The nearby Victorian tower with red terracotta decoration was used to supply hydraulic power to most of the south docks.

38__Della Robbia Room

Birkenhead shows its artistic side

Luca della Robbia was a famous Florentine Renaissance ceramic sculptor, but you will not see any of his work here. His name was borrowed by a small pottery company that opened in Birkenhead in 1894: in this room, at the Williamson Art Gallery and Museum, you will find the biggest collection anywhere of its eccentric wares.

The pieces reflect the character of the founder, Harold Rathbone, an artistic Liverpudlian who took his inspiration from William Morris and the Arts and Crafts movement. In Rathbone's pottery studio there was no machinery churning out identical objects: everything was made by hand using traditional methods, and the craftsmen and -women, mainly trained at local art schools, were encouraged to develop their own ideas. Rathbone lived in Hamilton Square, Birkenhead, which was lined with elegant houses. The pottery was just off the square, with the studio at 2a Price Street and the decorating and architectural departments at 28 Argyle Street (still a pottery).

Rathbone wanted to specialise in architectural ceramics; the firm made altarpieces for local churches and a grand fountain formerly in the courtyard of the Savoy Hotel, London, but smaller items – platters, vases, jugs, clock cases – sold better. Clients included royalty, Sarah Bernhardt, and Ignace Paderewski, and the pottery was sold through agents in New York, Paris, and London as well as in Liverpool.

The pots on display here show the typical della Robbia palette, dominated by pale greens, turquoise blues, and yellows. The usual decoration consisted of flowers, foliage, and fanciful Renaissance heads, often incised into the clay in flowing Art Nouveau lines. The firm's brief flowering was an exotic episode in a town devoted to shipbuilding and heavy industry. Rathbone was better at art than business; unable to combine the two, he closed the pottery in 1906.

Address Williamson Art Gallery and Museum, Slatey Road, Birkenhead CH43 4UE, Tel +44 1516524177, www.williamsonartgallery.org | **Getting there** Train to Birkenhead Hamilton Square, then a 10-minute taxi ride to Williamson Art Gallery; bus 471 or 472 from Liverpool, Sir Thomas Street to Birkenhead Central Library, then a 10-minute walk up Balls Road | **Hours** Wed–Sun 10am–5pm, closed Mon, Tue, and bank holidays | **Tip** Oxton Village, a short walk away, has characterful small shops and eateries.

39 __ Dream

The angel of the North West?

Just off the M 62 about halfway between Liverpool and Manchester, visible to thousands of motorists every day, is a gigantic white head, one of the most imaginative examples of public art in Britain. *Dream* is a 20-metre-high sculpture of a girl with her eyes closed, dreaming, and inviting us to dream with her. Her serene expression resembles a Buddha; the distorted shape of the head, stretched upwards, has an enigmatic realism. "When we dream, anything is possible," wrote its sculptor Jaume Plensa.

Located just outside the industrial town of St Helens, *Dream* is on the site of a spoil tip of Sutton Manor Colliery, which closed in 1991, the last of the local mines to be shut down. The scarred landscape has been planted with trees, and it is a pleasant ten-minute stroll up to the sculpture from the nearby road.

Made of precast concrete, the head has a sparkling white surface of Spanish dolomite, evoking the contrast with the blackness of the coal below, and embodying the motto *ex terra lucem* ("from the earth comes light"), of St Helens. The head rests on a round plinth inspired by the small circular tally carried by each miner as a means of identification.

Dream, completed in 2009, was the result of the Big Art Project, an ambitious scheme initiated by Channel 4 TV to involve local communities in creating public art. Sutton Manor was chosen as one of only seven locations in Britain to take part. A group of locals, including ex-miners, selected the Catalan sculptor Plensa, who worked closely with them. He initially proposed a gigantic miner's lamp, but they rejected it as too closely linked to the past. Plensa then suggested what had been his original idea, which he had thought they might find too challenging, a nine-year old girl dreaming about the future – her future and all our futures, an inspiration for generations to come.

Address Sutton Manor, St Helens WA 9 4BE, www.dreamsthelens.com | **Getting there**
Train from Lime Street to Lea Green station, then a 1-mile walk; bus 33 or 33A from
Lea Green station to Sutton Manor; by car, leave M 62 at junction 7, take A 57 towards
Warrington, turn left into B 5419 Jubits Lane, and park at King George V Sutton Manor
car park | **Tip** To the east of Sutton Manor is Clock Face Country Park, 57 acres of
woodlands, meadows, footpaths, and a fishing pond.

40___Duke's Terrace

Liverpool's sole surviving back-to-back terrace

Set behind Dukes and Duchesses Children's Nursery, on the east side of Duke Street, is a small three-storey terrace of 18 back-to-back houses of a type that was commonplace in Victorian Liverpool. Such dwellings were built to allow more people to be crammed in than the traditional terraces with yards and alleyways between them. Duke's Terrace dates from 1843 and was erected behind a group of Georgian town houses, which had been vacated by their wealthy owners. Originally the terrace was hidden from view, reached only by a basement passage from Duke Street.

Each house had a single room per floor; the cellar would originally have housed one family and was reached by an outside staircase. The floors above were occupied by a separate household, who would probably have had tenants. A pair of earth closets served each run of nine houses. As a single block, Duke's Terrace was only slightly better than the back-to-back housing that opened onto a narrow shared courtyard, which was the most insanitary form of housing in the city.

These appalling conditions led to Liverpool's appointment in 1847 of the country's first medical officer of health, Dr Duncan, who promptly enforced the closure of 5,000 cellar dwellings and later banned the construction of court housing. Yet, progress was slow, and in 1864, one fifth of the city's population still lived in courts, cellars, and back-to-back housing, comprising 22,000 homes. Even in 1914, some cellars were still inhabited, and the last courts were cleared only in the 1960s. The problem, like today, was an inadequate housing supply with private developers not building enough low-cost homes to provide decent housing for all.

Today it is difficult to imagine Duke's Terrace, which has been converted to nine rather than 18 dwellings, in its former sordid and smoke-blackened state.

Address Duke Street, Liverpool L 1 4JS | **Getting there** 8-minute walk from Central station | **Hours** The property is privately owned and gated; viewable only from the street | **Tip** On the opposite side of Duke Street is the well-established Italian restaurant Il Forno (No. 132), with its own olive oil and authentic Italian dishes.

41 Eleanor Rigby Statue

For "all the lonely people"

Inspired by John Lennon and Paul McCartney's song, the Eleanor Rigby statue depicts a woman sitting on a bench feeding a sparrow with a crust of bread. Almost faceless, she makes a pinched and pathetic figure, muffled up in her headscarf and bootees. It comes as a surprise to discover that the sculptor was Tommy Steele, the former teenage idol of the 1950s who made his name with covers of rock 'n' roll hits from the US charts. Steele later developed his career as a popular entertainer appearing in stage and film musicals all over the world.

In 1981 he was performing in Liverpool and offered to give the city a sculptural tribute to the Beatles. The city council accepted, hoping it would encourage visitors, and so Beatles Tourism was born. Steele charged just three pence for his work, an allusion to the musical *Half a Sixpence*, written as a showcase for his talents, and the *Liverpool Echo* paid for the piece to be cast in bronze (Steele sculpted a crumpled copy of the newspaper lying on the bench).

In his memoirs he recorded that he dropped several talismans into the molten bronze to endow the sculpture with magical properties: a four-leaf clover for good luck, a page from the Bible for spiritual help, a sonnet for lovers, an adventure book for excitement, and some old football socks for action. The magic must have worked, for *Eleanor Rigby* is held in great affection by locals and visitors alike. Many of them leave flowers and messages on the bench and have their photographs taken sitting next to her.

Eleanor sits in the shadow of the old post office, a grand Victorian building that was bombed in the blitz and was left empty for years until it opened as the Metquarter, a chic shopping centre. She is a figure from a previous age, when retail therapy was unknown. No designer clothes for her: out of her shopping bag peeps an old-fashioned milk bottle.

Address Stanley Street, Liverpool L1 6AL | **Getting there** 5-minute walk from James Street station | **Tip** Still in the mood for melancholy? Tucked away inside the Metquarter is *Grief*, a marble statue by Liverpool sculptor Herbert Tyson Smith commemorating 155 men and one woman, members of the Liverpool Post Office who died in World War I.

42 __ Eros the Second

See it better in Liverpool

Few of the tourists milling round the Eros fountain in Piccadilly Circus, London, know that there is another one in Liverpool. In Sefton Park, disturbed only by dog walkers, joggers, and mothers with baby buggies, you can appreciate the genius of the sculptor Alfred Gilbert in peace.

Look at Gilbert's weirdly inventive fantasy of writhing fish, shells, and merbabies. The sculpture seems to undulate with a life of its own, even when the water is turned off. It looks even better with water gushing out of the fishes' mouths and into the curved tank below. Above the fishes is an octagonal basin and an urn on a pedestal. Right at the top, perched on a nautilus shell, is the winged figure of Eros. Most of the fountain is made of bronze, but Eros himself is aluminium. Gilbert was one of the first sculptors to use this new material, taking advantage of its lightness and tensile strength: the figure's pose – resting on one leg on tiptoe, as if about to take off – would not have been possible in bronze.

The Liverpool Eros, made in 1932, is a replica of the one in London, which was unveiled in 1893 as a memorial to the philanthropist Lord Shaftesbury. Although called Eros, the Greek god of sexual love, the winged figure actually represents his twin brother Anteros, the god of returned love, symbolising Shaftesbury's selfless commitment to the poor. George Audley, an art-loving Liverpool businessman, so admired the London landmark that he commissioned Gilbert to make the second version. Audley also donated a replica of another famous London sculpture to Sefton Park: the Peter Pan statue near the Palm House.

By the 1990s, the fountain had become badly corroded. The bronze parts were repaired, but Eros himself was replaced by a totally new aluminium figure in 2008, and so is a replica of a replica. The "original" has been preserved by National Museums Liverpool.

Address Sefton Park, Liverpool L17 1AP | **Getting there** 20-minute walk from St Michael's station; bus 82 from Liverpool One bus station to Dingle, Allington Street, then a 15-minute walk; enter Sefton Park via Lark Lane | **Tip** Contemplate Eros from the terrace of the nearby cafe while sipping coffee or eating an ice cream.

43__Everton Tower
The lit-up lock-up

This delightful small round building with a conical top is now all that is left of the vanished village of Everton, before it was swallowed up by Liverpool. Built in 1787, the lock-up was used to hold drunks and petty criminals overnight, before they were taken for trial the morning after. Nearby was the famous Everton Toffee Shop (suppliers to Queen Victoria and Charles Dickens), and in 1879, at a meeting held in a hotel in the village, St Domingo's football team, founded the previous year, decided to change its name to Everton Football Club.

As Liverpool expanded, the rustic character of the village changed. First wealthy merchants built mansions here, then the area was covered in working-class terraced housing, and with the slum clearance of the 1960s came 25 tower blocks, nicknamed the Piggeries. In the 1980s, most of the tower blocks were demolished and Everton Heights was cleared to make an extensive park. Recently, colourful wildflower meadows have been planted marking the sites of three of Everton's vanished streets.

Today the lock-up stands in the park with a magnificent view of Liverpool as a backdrop. Landmarks on the skyline include both cathedrals, the turrets of Lime Street station, the Wellington Column, the Royal Liver Building, the skyscrapers of modern Liverpool, and the tobacco warehouse. There are glimpses of the Mersey and Birkenhead, the hills of North Wales are visible in the distance, and the foreground is animated by revolving wind turbines. Views farther out to sea can be had from higher up the hillside.

Village lock-ups fell out of use in the Victorian period as local police stations were built. Many have been demolished, but the Everton Lock-Up has been lucky: Everton Football Club made it part of its official crest in 1938 and, more recently, contributed to the cost of its restoration. Now, every night, it is floodlit in blue.

Address Village Street, Everton, Liverpool L 5 4LS | **Getting there** Buses from Queen Square bus station: 14 to Everton Road; 21 or 242 to Netherfield Road/Everton Brow | **Tip** A little further down the hill, off Prince Edwin Street, watch the action at the glow-in-the-dark skateboard park designed by South Korean artist Koo Jeong A.

44 Festival Gardens
Japan-on-Merseyside

The Festival Gardens were constructed in response to the Toxteth riots of 1981. These uprisings, prompted by poverty and unemployment among young people in Liverpool, shocked the nation. The idea of an international garden festival came from the flamboyant environment minister Michael Heseltine, who was appointed "Minister for Liverpool" with a mission to turn the city's failing economy around. The event was based on the Bundesgartenschau horticultural shows in Germany, and was intended to showcase the city and develop civic pride.

The festival occupied an industrial wasteland overlooking the River Mersey, and involved the creation of 60 individual gardens with 30 countries participating. Running from May to October 1984 and attracting 3.8 million visitors, it was hailed as a huge success. After the festival was over, the site was sold for housing and recreation, but in spite of ambitious development plans, little was done and it soon became an overgrown jungle. A rich ecosystem developed with a mix of flora and fauna, which still inhabit the area.

Only now, following years of neglect, has this sleeping beauty started to come alive again. Amazingly, the showpiece of the festival, the Japanese garden, survived, and after clearance of dense vegetation, replanting, and the rebuilding of the wooden rest house – which had been burned to the ground – the beauty and refinement of the original design was recaptured. Nearby is the Chinese garden, with a lake, waterfall, and two pagodas, their roofs now repaired with 5,000 decorative tiles imported from China.

The current transformation is letting the gardens breathe once more. Largely carried out by volunteers, work has continued slowly on the rest of the land, and now there is new optimism: the city council has repurchased the festival site, with big plans for cultural and community events.

Address Riverside Drive, Liverpool L 17 5BU, www.liverpoolfestivalgardens.com | **Getting there** Bus 82A from Liverpool One bus station to St Michael's station, then a 5-minute walk | **Hours** Nov–Mar, daily 8:30am–4pm; Apr, daily 8:30am–6pm; May–Sept, daily 8:30am–6pm; Oct, daily 8:30am–6pm | **Tip** Otterspool Promenade, reachable from the Festival Gardens, is an attractive riverside walk from Otterspool Park to Garston Docks.

45 __ Florence Institute

Where Gerry Marsden learned to play the guitar

Ten years ago, the Florence Institute was a roofless ruin, boarded up and abandoned. Dating from 1889, it was built by Bernard Hill, a wealthy merchant and mayor of Liverpool, in memory of his daughter Florence, who died in Paris aged 22. Affectionately known by locals as the Florrie, it was the first purpose-built youth club in Britain, providing recreation and instruction for poor and young working lads of the Dingle, a tough dockside area of the city. Generations of boys took up sports and hobbies at the Florrie, including boxing heroes Dick Tiger, Larry Paul, and Alan Rudkin. Gerry Marsden, who learned to play the guitar at the Florrie, went on to form Gerry and the Pacemakers, whose 1960s hit songs included "Ferry Cross the Mersey" and "You'll Never Walk Alone," the anthem of the Liverpool Football Club.

During Liverpool's economic decline, the youth club was dissolved and in 1988, the building closed, passing by default to the Duchy of Lancaster (part of the Queen's estate). A major fire destroyed the roof in 1999 and appeared to mark the building's end. Yet from the ashes arose a phoenix: locals began a determined campaign and, with support from the Bishop of Liverpool and city council leaders, raised a sum of £6.3 million for its restoration.

On 21 January, 2013, the Prince of Wales reopened the Florrie. Five years prior, he had paid the derelict Florrie a visit: when he asked who owned the complex, he learned to his amazement that it belonged to his mother. Now the Florence Institute is once again the focal point of the community, with a 300-seat auditorium, a gym, cafe, crèche, library, and heritage centre. It is open seven days a week, and if you don't fancy joining a dance group or an art class, take a look at the glorious interior, resplendent in decorative tilework and stained glass. You will see that nothing was too good for the Dingle lads.

Address 377 Mill Street, Liverpool L 8 4RF, Tel +44 1517282323, www.theflorrie.org |
Getting there 10-minute walk from Brunswick station; bus 130 from the Strand to Mill
Street, Dingle | **Hours** Mon–Sat 9am–6pm, Sun 10am–4pm | **Tip** Ringo Starr, another
Dingle lad, was born at 9 Madryn Street, a 10-minute walk from the Florrie.

46 __ Fort Perch Rock

Maritime fort with a quirky museum collection

Here is a real fort, built out into the sea, where you can view a random collection of relics from military and maritime disasters. Fort Perch Rock was erected to defend the seaward passage into the Port of Liverpool after the Napoleonic Wars. When completed, in 1829, it was equipped with a 15-gun battery, which was periodically updated until the introduction of machine guns at the turn of the 20th century. During World War II, the concrete turrets were added to the tops of the bastions and it served as a radar station. To fool enemy airmen, it was made to look like a tea garden, with a large "TEAS" sign displayed on the roof and the fortifications painted green like a lawn. On only two occasions did the fort go into action. The first was at the outbreak of World War I, when a shot was fired across the bow of a Norwegian sailing ship whose skipper was unaware that war had been declared. The second was at the outbreak of World War II, when a small fishing boat received similar treatment, allowing the fort commander to claim the first British shot fired, just 15 minutes after war was declared.

In 1956, the fort passed into private ownership and now functions as a museum. It contains a strange collection of objects, mostly connected with the two world wars. The centrepiece is a display of crashed aircraft parts – British, American, and German – recovered from sites across the UK. The tragic story is told of the loss of submarine HMS *Thetis*, built at Cammell Laird's Birkenhead shipyard. There is a re-creation of the radio room on the *Titanic*, and a huge model of HMS *Prince of Wales*, one of the last great battleships, which was launched in the Mersey and sunk off the coast of Singapore in 1941. To finish off, you can brush up on the meeting in Los Angeles between Elvis and the Beatles, with accompanying memorabilia exploring Wirral's part in the Merseybeat scene.

Address Marine Promenade, New Brighton, Wirral CH45 2JU, Tel +44 7976282120, www.fortperchrock.org | **Getting there** Train to New Brighton station, then a 10-minute walk | **Tip** If you fancy a bracing walk to the top of the hill, the landmark "Dome of Home" is a shrine church dedicated to Saints Peter, Paul, and Philomena, where the Latin Mass is celebrated (open daily, www.domeofhome.org).

47___Fountain in Williamson Square

Watery words by a Liverpool poet

In 1965 the American beat poet Allen Ginsburg declared Liverpool "the centre of consciousness of the human universe." He said the same about Milwaukee and Baltimore, but we'll let that pass: Liverpool in the sixties was certainly fizzing with creativity. In 1967 the Beatles released *Sgt. Pepper's Lonely Hearts Club Band*, and Penguin Modern Poets published *The Mersey Sound*, an anthology of poems by Adrian Henri, Brian Patten, and Roger McGough. It went on to sell more than a million copies.

Of the three Liverpool poets, only McGough achieved national fame: a broadcaster, playwright, and children's author as well as a poet, he writes in a way that is always accessible, and with typical Liverpool humour. His poem *Water* was commissioned by the city for the fountain in Williamson Square. The words are set into the paving around the fountain so that the poem can be started from any point: "…water is mischievous is fidgety is chatterbox / water is Liverpool is river is paradox." McGough wanted the poem to sound like a playground rhyme. But it is the water, not *Water*, that is a hit with children, who scream with delight, daring each other to run through the tunnels formed by the arched jets rising and falling out of the pavement: "water is fountainous is gymnast is flash / water is mountainous is scallywag is splash …"

The fountain, installed in 2004, has brought new life to the square. The 20 jets, circulating 37,000 litres every two hours, are controlled by a computer from an underground pump room. In the evening, the water is lit up in changing colours, and later there is a misting effect.

There used to be two theatres here: the Theatre Royal is no more, but the Playhouse is still flourishing, its bold extension of interlocking cylinders further evidence of Liverpool's creativity in the sixties.

Address Williamson Square, Liverpool L1 1EQ | **Getting there** 5-minute walk from Lime Street station or Central station; 2-minute walk from Queen Square bus station | **Tip** Just off the square is the Royal Court theatre (1 Roe Street), an Art Deco building where uproarious Scouse comedies are a speciality.

48 Freedom! Sculpture

Campaigning against slavery then and now

The first thing you see in the Slavery Museum is a striking assemblage of rusty metal and flashing lights, made out of recycled car parts and discarded machinery. The Freedom! sculpture, commissioned to celebrate the 200th anniversary of the abolition of the slave trade in 2007, was created by Haitian artists Eugene, Celeur, Guyodo, and Mario Benjamin working with youth groups from the slums of Port-Au-Prince. The same year saw the opening of the International Slavery Museum in Liverpool on Slavery Remembrance Day, observed on the anniversary of the uprising of enslaved Africans in Haiti on August 23, 1791.

The Freedom! sculpture expresses anger, pride, intensity, suffering, and hope all at the same time. It is about history, and it is about now: Haiti became the first black republic, but is today one of the poorest countries in the world. In this museum, history is not something in the past, sealed off from the present. The displays about Liverpool's role in the transatlantic slave trade are compelling: paintings and models of slave ships; shackles and restraints; a re-creation of a plantation; portraits of slave owners; testimonies about the brutal treatment of slaves; objects decorated with abolitionist motifs. The museum also tells a much bigger story, about colonialism and racial prejudice, and about campaigns of resistance such as the Civil Rights movement. You can listen to jazz and blues and see portraits of black achievers, from Muhammad Ali to Benjamin Zephaniah. Crucially, the final section is about the persistence of slavery, inequality, and racism today.

The new museum, which started as a pioneering display in the Maritime Museum, is expanding. By acquiring the dock traffic office next door with its imposing entrance, the International Slavery Museum has gained more space for display, study, and education, distinguishing it as a centre of activism and debate.

Address International Slavery Museum, Dock Traffic Office, Albert Dock, Liverpool L 3 4AX, Tel +44 1514784499, www.liverpoolmuseums.org.uk/ism | **Getting there** 5-minute walk from James Street station | **Hours** Daily 10am–5pm, closed Dec 24 from 2pm, Dec 25–26, and Jan 1 | **Tip** By the side of Tate Liverpool (Albert Dock) is *Raleigh*, two trumpet-like forms lying on top of granite and cast-iron dock bollards, by Liverpool-born sculptor Tony Cragg.

49 _ Granby Four Streets

Winner of the Turner Prize

Four streets of terraced housing in Granby are hardly the stuff of tourist brochures, yet they have seen a remarkable coming together of housing renewal, urban greening, and art. A few years ago the area was all but derelict: now many houses have been restored and are lived in, while others are clad in scaffolding for repairs. Even amidst the graffiti and boarded-up windows, trees and pots of flowers flourish; perched on windowsills and roofs are coloured pigeons created by artist Patrick Murphy to represent marginalised groups.

Granby, deprived, ethnically diverse, and home to Scousers as well as immigrants from Somalia and Yemen, was a lively community until many of its terraced streets were demolished in the name of regeneration. Bland and inappropriate suburban-style homes were built to replace the terraces, but four streets were left untouched. Empty houses stood abandoned, but a few residents hung on. They campaigned, they cleaned and painted, they planted flowers, they installed picnic tables for communal meals, and eventually their persistence paid off.

A new Community Land Trust brought together a range of bodies to share the financial risk of refurbishment: housing associations, social investors, artists' collectives, architects, and residents. Gradually they are raising funds to bring the houses back into use. The Granby Workshops make doorknobs, fireplaces, and tiles, and provide training and employment opportunities linked to the project. Future plans include the renovation of four empty corner shops and the creation of a winter garden, an attraction for visitors as well as residents.

The artists' collective Assemble won the 2015 Turner prize for its work on the four streets. For the Turner prize judges, the award may have been about giving art a new social purpose; for the locals, it was about Assemble actually listening to their views.

Address Beaconsfield, Cairns, Jermyn, and Ducie streets, Liverpool L8 2XA | **Getting there** Bus 27, 75, or 80 from Liverpool One bus station to Princes Park gates | **Hours** 24/7. Street market: Apr–Sept, first Sat every month; Christmas market: first Sat in Dec | **Tip** Lodge Lane Superstore nearby is an award-winning shop selling an immense range of cheap fresh fruit, vegetables, and exotic ingredients from around the world.

50 Hilbre Island

Walk on water to a peaceful nature reserve

Hilbre Island is the largest of three red sandstone outcrops in the mouth of the Dee Estuary, which separates the Wirral peninsula from Wales. If you take note of the tide times, it can be safely reached on foot from West Kirby (a distance of two miles across the wet sands) three hours before and after low water. The island takes its name from St Hildeburgh, who is thought to have lived there as a hermit in the 7th century, and it became a place of pilgrimage in the Middle Ages. Later, when Chester was a major port, the island boasted a custom house and an inn, but these activities were abandoned when the River Dee silted up and maritime trade diverted to Liverpool. Although a few buildings remain, including a former buoy master's house and a telegraph station, nobody lives on the island today, which has an isolated and lonely feel.

Hilbre's special appeal is its fauna and flora. It is a nature reserve, and you can spend your time searching for sea lavender and other coastal plants, poking about in rock pools, or watching the antics of grey seals, which sun themselves on the sandbanks and swim in the surrounding shallow waters (the seals are just as interested in humankind as we are in them).

The Dee Estuary is one of the ten most significant estuaries in Europe for migrating waders and wildfowl. They feed on the marshes and sandbanks, and roost on the island when the mud flats are covered by the tide. Founded in 1957, the Hilbre Bird Observatory records the birds overwintering in the estuary, and posts photos and reports sightings on a daily blog (www.hilbrebirdobs.blogspot.co.uk). Common species include oystercatcher, curlew, and the colourful shelduck, which feed on the mud; rarer are the purple sandpiper, Manx shearwater, and storm petrel. The island offers fresh air and simple pleasures, but don't leave the return trip too late or you will be up to your neck in water.

Address Hilbre Island, Wirral CH48 8BW, www.deeestuary.co.uk/hilbre | **Getting there**
Wirral line train to West Kirby. Start from Dee Lane slipway next to the Marine Lake.
Walk towards Little Eye, the smallest of the three islands, then turn right to Middle Eye
and on to Hilbre Island. | **Hours** Generally safe to cross up to 3 hours before and after
low tide: www.tidetimes.org.uk/hilbre-island-tide-times | **Tip** After the walk, treat yourself
at the 1386 Deli, purveyors of fine Portuguese food and wine, at 27 Grange Road, just
next to the station.

51 Holt's Arcade

New York style

The elegant shopping arcade that connects Water and Brunswick streets could be in New York. It marks the route of a narrow lane that was subsumed when the vast India Buildings project was constructed over it in the 1920s. Designed by architect Herbert J. Rowse, it was built for the shipping firm Alfred Holt & Co, owner of the Blue Funnel Line. Rowse went on to design the Philharmonic Hall and the Mersey Tunnel, but the India Buildings was his first major commission. After studying at Liverpool University, he worked in New York and Chicago, where he saw the skyscrapers that inspired India Buildings.

The mix of tenants that first occupied it was also characteristic of American city blocks: a bank, post office, insurance companies, and government offices, as well as a public hall and a club. The arcade, which is lined in polished travertine and surmounted by a tunnel vault decorated in green and gold, has its original elevator doors, kiosks with bronze shop fronts selling newspapers and confectionery, a hairdresser with original 1930s furnishings, a gents' tailor, and a seller of Art Deco curios.

In 2013, the building was found to have been the subject of one of the UK's biggest-ever frauds. For five years, the then owner, a Greek shipping tycoon, had used forged documents to cheat the Irish Allied Bank and the Bank of Scotland out of a total of £760 million, including the purchase and running costs of India Buildings. During the trial the jury was told how Achilleas Kallakis had used the proceeds to fund a lifestyle of chauffeur-driven Bentleys, a private jet, and a luxury yacht moored at Monaco. Kallakis and his business partner were jailed for seven and five years respectively, and India Buildings, which suffered serious mismanagement during this period, has since struggled to regain its position as one of the city's most prestigious addresses.

Address India Buildings, 31 Water Street, Liverpool L2 0RD | **Getting there** 3-minute walk from James Street station. A pedestrian tunnel (open Mon–Fri 7am–10am and 3pm–6pm) entered at platform level, passes beneath India Buildings and exits into Water Street. | **Hours** Mon–Sat 9am–5pm | **Tip** On the other side of Water Street is Rowse's masterpiece, the former Martin's Bank. Inside is one of the finest banking halls in the country (currently closed), complete with Art Deco furnishings. During World War II, its vault housed most of Britain's gold reserves.

52 Hornby Library

A temple to the art of the book

The Hornby Library, tucked away at the back of Central Library, used to be an inner sanctum where only the privileged were allowed. No longer. Since 2013, when the building was remodelled, the sanctum has been open to all.

Hornby, a Victorian merchant, bequeathed his rare books to the city, together with money to house them. His library, opened in 1906, is an ornate but intimate room in the Edwardian Baroque style lined with glass-fronted bookcases of bibliographical rarities. The collection has since been expanded to over 15,000 rare books and bindings and 8,000 prints, and includes such items as the city's Charter of 1207, granted by King John, a letter signed by Queen Elizabeth I, and the sketches made by Edward Lear on his first visit to Italy.

There is a programme of changing exhibitions but the greatest treasure of all is always on view. In the adjoining Oak Room is an enormous showcase displaying a copy of Audubon's *Birds of America*, comprising 435 large hand-coloured engravings, published between 1827 and 1838. Audubon created striking designs out of the birds' elegant shapes and vividly coloured plumage, yet he also set new standards of realism, depicting the birds as life-size and in their natural habitats – feeding, flying, nesting, or fighting for prey. The pages are turned weekly, but a nearby touch screen allows all the illustrations to be viewed.

Only 120 copies of the large-size edition are known to have survived, and based on its sale price at auction, today it is the world's most expensive book. The city bought its copy in 1860 for £165. Liverpool played a crucial role in the book's history. Audubon could not raise the money to publish it in America, and came to Europe to drum up funds. He began in 1826 in Liverpool, where the philanthropists William Rathbone and William Roscoe were among the first to subscribe.

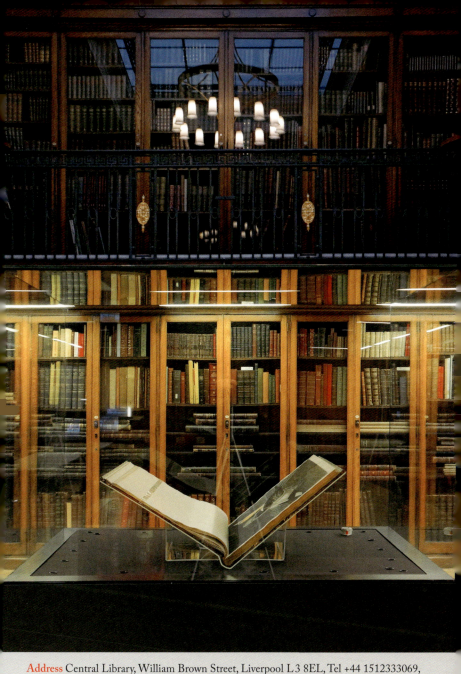

Address Central Library, William Brown Street, Liverpool L3 8EL, Tel +44 1512333069, www.liverpool.gov.uk/libraries | **Getting there** 5-minute walk from Lime Street station or Queen Square bus station | **Hours** Mon–Fri 9am–8pm, Sat 9am–5pm, Sun 10am–5pm | **Tip** When you enter the Central Library, look upwards. You will be surprised. There is also a fabulous view of the city from the roof terrace.

53 — Hoylake and West Kirby War Memorial

Monument with a view of the River Dee

Tommy (short for Tommy Atkins) is slang for the ordinary British soldier, and it is the courage of the Tommies in the First World War that is celebrated in this memorial, a colossal granite obelisk on a commanding hilltop site above West Kirby with a sweeping view across the Dee Estuary to North Wales. The monument has two larger-than-life bronze figures by the sculptor Charles Sargeant Jagger, best known for his Royal Artillery Memorial at Hyde Park Corner. Most World War I memorials gloss over the horror of the conflict with high-minded idealism or abstraction, but those by Jagger typically feature grimly realistic portrayals of soldiers.

The soldier "on defence" so vividly represented at West Kirby is an infantryman, dishevelled but resolute. Dressed for winter, his helmet pushed to the back of his head, he stands guard, with rifle, gas mask, and water bottle. At his feet lies a German helmet. Above is written, "Who stands if freedom falls. Who dies if England live." On the other side of the monument is a more conventional figure of a hooded woman holding a baby and a wreath of thorns entwined with poppies, with broken manacles dangling from her wrists. Standing on a globe, she represents Humanity breaking the shackles of war.

Jagger's depiction of soldiers was based on first-hand knowledge, for he had seen active service as an infantry officer. Wounded twice, in Gallipoli and France, he was awarded the Military Cross. "Experience in the trenches persuaded me of the necessity for frankness and truth," he wrote. Although the monument was created to commemorate the men and women from Hoylake and West Kirby who lost their lives in the Great War, text has been added to include those who died in World War II, and in the wars in Korea, Cyprus, Iraq, and Afghanistan.

WHO STANDS IF

TO THE MEN AND WOMEN FROM
THESE PARTS WHO LAID DOWN
THEIR LIVES IN THE GREAT WAR
1914 – 1919 – 1939 –1945

THEY WERE A WALL UNTO US
BOTH BY NIGHT AND DAY.

Address Grange Hill, West Kirby CH14 4ET | **Getting there** Train from Lime Street station to West Kirby station, then a 10-minute walk up Grange Hill, left turn into Grange Old Road, footpath signed to War Memorial; by car to West Kirby, park in Grange Old Road | **Tip** Go for a walk round Marine Lake at West Kirby, popular for sailing and canoeing.

54__John Lewis Pedestrian Bridge

An architectural twist

A gravity-defying structure twists and turns over the busy entrance to the Canning Place bus exchange: it is a high-level bridge linking the Liver Street multi-storey car park with the John Lewis store at Liverpool One. With a span of over 70 meters, it is believed to be the longest box bridge in the world, relying on an ingenious system of steel plates and ribs, concealed behind the smooth surfaces of the metal tube, for strength.

As you walk across the bridge, the glazed slots in the roof and walls provide fascinating views of the Albert Dock and the riverfront on the one side and the Anglican Cathedral and Radio City Tower on the other. Below you is the continuous movement of buses. Moreover, the twists in the walkway produce shortened sightlines, and the angles at which light is admitted create optical illusions. At night, translucent glass panels within the tube glow in soft red and blue light, reflecting the colours of the city's two famous football clubs. When the weather is stormy, the structure sways gently, giving the vague impression of being at sea. The bridge is also intriguing to view from below, where the complex zigzag geometry brings to mind the beauty of origami, the Japanese art of paper folding.

Wilkinson Eyre, the architects for the bridge, also designed the nearby Arena and Conference Centre on the waterfront. This has a fluidly curved body reminiscent of a massive oyster shell, and contrasts with the regimented form of the Albert Dock alongside. Though the bridge is visually different from the arena complex, it too is a highly engineered structure contained in an outer skin. Contemporary architecture like the bridge not only makes the city's streets more exciting, but also serves to re-establish Liverpool's industrial tradition of pioneering, innovative design.

Address Liver Street Q Park, Liverpool L 1 8LJ | **Getting there** 2-minute walk from Liverpool One bus station; 8-minute walk from James Street station | **Hours** Mon–Fri 9:30am–8pm, Sat 9am–7pm, Sun 11am–5pm (John Lewis store opening hours) | **Tip** At the end of Hanover Street, outside John Lewis, is a set of decorative sea-themed iron gates, all that remains of the magnificent Sailors' Home, which stood nearby.

55 __ K6 Telephone Box

The smallest inside the largest

When the architect Giles Gilbert Scott won the competition to build Liverpool's Anglican Cathedral in 1903 at the age of 22, his only constructed design was a pipe rack. Upon completion, 75 years later, his magnificent neo-Gothic cathedral became England's largest, vying with St John the Divine in New York City to be the largest Protestant cathedral in the world. What is not so well known is that Scott also designed one of the smallest buildings ever to be erected: the red telephone box, once found throughout every town and village in Britain.

He designed the K6, as it is known, in 1935, and there is one still to be found inside Liverpool Cathedral, tucked into a corner at the top of the stairs that connect the nave with the undercroft below. Scott's inspiration for his box came from the 18th-century architect John Soane, who was fascinated by the use of pendentives, the four concave triangular weight-bearing elements that support a dome above a square space. One of the earliest and most exceptional examples of pendentives is in the construction of the dome of the 6th-century church of Hagia Sophia, in Constantinople. By comparison, Scott's creation is miniscule; pendentives for him were a means of giving his small but perfectly formed telephone box a touch of elegance that would make it fit into any urban or rural location in Britain without looking out of place. The bright red paint is the livery of the General Post Office, which was responsible for UK telecommunications until 1969, when it was abolished.

Remarkably, this utilitarian object has become a much-loved ornament: most of those K6 telephone boxes that survive in the age of the mobile phone are now listed buildings. Giles Gilbert Scott also designed the Battersea Power Station in London: it is a tribute to his architectural genius that he was the master of the small as well as the big.

Address Liverpool Cathedral, St James's Mount, Liverpool L1 7AZ, www.liverpoolcathedral.org.uk | **Getting there** 15-minute walk from Central station; CityLink bus from Liverpool One bus station to Upper Duke Street | **Hours** Daily 8am–6pm, except Christmas Day 8am–3pm | **Tip** Tours of the Cathedral tower with stunning panoramas include views of the bells and the Elizabeth Hoare Gallery of ecclesiastical embroidery.

56 Kitty Wilkinson Statue
Her-story is made

St George's Hall expresses the confidence of Victorian Liverpool. Inside, the granite columns, marble balconies, bronze doors, glittering lamps and sumptuous tiles recall the wealth and power of Imperial Rome. The building was used for concerts and assemblies, but like the Roman Pantheon, it was also intended to honour great citizens. Around the edge of the Great Hall are 26 niches, but until recently only 12 were filled with statues, and all of them men – peers, statesmen, politicians, clerics, intellectuals.

History was made in 2012 when the first statue of a female Liverpudlian was unveiled in one of the empty spaces, hopefully to be followed by others such as Josephine Butler and Eleanor Rathbone. The new statue represents Kitty Wilkinson, a working-class woman whose role in the 1832 cholera epidemic led to the provision of public wash houses. While tending the sick, she offered the use of her kitchen as a wash house, and with the advice of a surgeon, began to wash and disinfect bedding. As a result of her example, Liverpool opened its first public wash house in 1842, where the poor could have a bath and clean their clothes and linen at minimal cost. Other towns and cities followed suit.

It was a controversial idea to commission a modern statue for such an important interior, and dire predictions were made. After a competition, the job was awarded to sculptor Simon Smith, who works in marble in a traditional style. He had very little to go on, as the only known picture of Wilkinson is a small photograph. His statue fits in well with the others, but he still managed to make it subtly subversive. The male figures stand relaxed and supremely self-confident of their place in the world, but Wilkinson looks entirely practical. A pile of sheets is at her feet, and whereas the men are static, she is rolling up her sleeves, determined to get on with the washing.

CATHERINE WILKINSON
1786–1860

Address St George's Hall, St George's Plateau, Liverpool L 1 1JJ, Tel +44 1512333020, www.liverpoolcityhalls.co.uk/st-georges-hall | **Getting there** 2-minute walk from Lime Street station; 3-minute walk from Queen Square bus station | **Hours** Daily 10am–4pm, closed Christmas and New Year's Day | **Tip** St John's Gardens, at the back of St George's Hall, is a pleasant place to sit on a warm day, and there are plenty more statues (all male).

57___Lark Lane

Shabby chic and first-rate food

Lark Lane is a great place for mooching and lunching. It is a friendly street of shops and eateries with buildings in a variety of styles. The gothic police station, in red brick with an impressive stone gryphon, is Victorian; it is now home to Phil's Picture Palace (selling all things framed), Little Miss Seamstress, and Blessing Natural Therapies. Slightly later in date is the building housing Maranto's Restaurant, featuring a tall black-and-white projecting window bay with a gabled roof and clock. It was originally the Christ Church Institute, built in 1884.

Several shops retain their old fronts: the ghostly lettering of Hiram Crew, Saddler, and Harness Maker lingers on above Paul's, an old-fashioned barber. A more recent arrival is the self-consciously retro Scraggs Barbershop, with Fallen Angel Tattoos upstairs. Retro is a bit of a theme on Lark Lane: you can try on a pair of Dame Edna-style sunglasses at Larks, a quirky vintage and contemporary gift shop, browse for antiques in Remains to be Seen, or rummage through 1950s kitsch furniture at Gasp, down Lucerne Street.

If it is drink you are after, there is Bier, offering more than 100 world beers, or the Albert, with its unspoiled Victorian interior: prop yourself up on the wonderfully solid wooden bar and admire the two enormous wooden barrels above the rows of bottles. As for restaurants, there is a huge choice: Thai, Indian, Caribbean, Greek, Spanish, several Turkish barbecues, and a Moroccan bistro that is also a bazaar. Other options include Moon and Pea, which also has a deli selling delicious picnic hampers; Bistro Rhubarb, where you'll find a good club sandwich with proper chips; or On the Pallet, with its stylish interior. Finish off with an ice cream from Gelato or a slab of tiffin from Balbero's Buffet Platters, and wander off through the gateway at the end of the street into Sefton Park for a snooze on the grass.

Address Lark Lane, Liverpool L17 8US, between Sefton Park and Aigburth Road |
Getting there 15-minute walk from St Michael's station; bus 82 from Liverpool One bus
station to Dingle, Allington Street | **Tip** Just off Lark Lane is Hadassah Grove (*hassadah*
is Hebrew for myrtle), a peaceful enclave of early-19th-century houses and overgrown
gardens exuding an air of pleasing decay.

58__Leaf

Teabags not allowed

For years sales of tea have been declining as coffee has captured the taste buds of the public. But at Leaf, tea drinking has become hip. The atmosphere is relaxed. There are young people, old people, families – on summer evenings patrons spill out onto the pavement and the hubbub of conversation dominates.

More than 50 varieties of tea are on the menu – white, black, green, rooibos, and herbal – with blends as exotic as Heaven Scent (white peony with added lemongrass, ginkgo, coconut, and pineapple) or as homely as English Breakfast (a medium-bodied mix of black teas from India and Ceylon). There is not a teabag in sight: teabags, Leaf's owners tell us, "consist of smaller pieces of tea leaves or tea fanning, basically dust," whereas loose tea has a better flavour. But tea is only the beginning. Leaf is also a great place to eat. Plenty of delicious cakes and scones, of course, but also imaginative dishes made with wholesome ingredients: perhaps some cinnamon porridge with jam and toasted nuts for breakfast, or a fish sharing platter with focaccia and saffron aioli for lunch. There's more still: events include films, life drawing classes, and Retro Sundays with vintage fairs. Out of the Bedroom on Tuesdays provides a platform for young musicians to perform, and on First Listen Fridays a favourite new album is played from start to finish. The monthly Pudding Club serves five (yes, five) desserts accompanied by specially selected teas.

The decor is as eccentric as the concept: branches of trees, twinkling lights, and chintzy fringed lampshades dangle from the ceiling, and you can sit on squashy armchairs and chesterfields or wooden chairs at marble-topped tables. In the evening Leaf becomes a bar with live music but you can still order a cup of tea. Their motto is, "You can't buy happiness but you can buy tea, and that's kind of the same thing."

Address 65–67 Bold Street, Liverpool L1 4EZ, Tel +44 1517077747, www.thisisleaf.co.uk |
Getting there 5-minute walk from Central station | **Hours** Mon–Thu 9am–midnight,
Fri 9am–2am, Sat 10am–2am, Sun 10am–midnight | **Tip** See a film at nearby FACT
(88 Wood Street), the film and media arts centre where the Garden, a vegetarian eatery, is
run by Leaf.

59 Lime Street Rock Cutting

Outstanding feat of railway engineering

All trains approaching Lime Street station pass through a spectacular deep canyon with sheer rock sides. If you peer upwards from the train window, you will see bridges carrying the city's streets, and the occasional building perched high above. Shafts of sunlight penetrate the gloom, allowing glimpses into dark underground chambers and illuminating the names of the streets passing overhead. It is a memorable introduction to the city.

But this rock cutting is just one important contribution made by Liverpool to early railway history. The Liverpool and Manchester Railway, constructed by the engineer and inventor George Stephenson, was the world's first passenger-train system, opening in 1830. Originally it terminated outside the city centre at Crown Street, before being extended, six years later, to Lime Street through a 1.1-mile rock tunnel. At first, outbound carriages were hauled up the steep incline by cable. This system was replaced by locomotives in 1879. But smoke within the tunnel proved to be a problem, and in 1881, work was begun on slicing spaces through the bedrock to open it up to fresh air. Seven short lengths of tunnel were retained to support the web of streets and buildings above, and bridges were built across the chasm.

Trains enter the cutting via an archway at Edge Hill station into a short section of the 1836 tunnel (the oldest rail tunnel still in use in the world). Another archway alongside leads into the Waterloo Tunnel of 1848, which runs for 2.07 miles below the city to the north docks, and took emigrants to the former Riverside station for their voyage to the New World. A third archway is the entrance to the earlier Wapping Tunnel of 1830, which leads to the south docks. Neither the Wapping nor Waterloo tunnel is now in use; but both remain in good condition and could surely be given new life in a future transport scheme for the city.

Address Edge Hill station, Tunnel Road, Liverpool L 7 6ND | **Getting there** You can see into the cutting from the far end of Platform 9 at Lime Street station or from the platforms at Edge Hill, but you get the best view from the train as it slows down just before arrival at Lime Street | **Tip** On arrival at Lime Street station, try Wetherspoon's Pub in the former North Western Hotel, accessible from the concourse. Its four bars are decorated with vintage railway and steamship posters and photographs.

60 Liver Birds
Here, there, and everywhere

What rare bird can be seen roosting on buildings all over the city, but never in flight? Answer: the Liver bird, the emblem of Liverpool. The closest it gets to flying is when perched, with wings outspread and a sprig of seaweed in its beak, on the twin towers of the Royal Liver Building. Yet legend has it that should the birds ever fly away, the city would cease to exist.

The origins of the civic symbol have been much contested. In the Middle Ages, the town used an eagle on its seal, but later, its shape was changed – possibly due to incompetent draughtsmanship – into a cormorant, also known as a leaver, making an unintended play on the name of Liverpool. Over the years, further confusion arose as it was depicted in a variety of forms, with long legs or short legs, webbed feet or talons, resembling anything "from a goose to a long-necked heron" as one historian put it. Those creatures atop the Liver Building, bearing little resemblance to any known species, have brilliantly promoted the myth of a fabulous bird that once inhabited the Pool inlet.

When completed, in 1910, the Liver Building was the tallest commercial building in Britain, hailed as the country's first skyscraper. The gigantic Liver birds are three times as tall as a man. They were made of copper sheets around a steel frame by the Bromsgrove Guild of Craftsmen, reputedly to the design of the sculptor Carl Bernard Bartels. Originally the birds were gilded, but despite the erection of a windbreak when the gold leaf was applied, twice as much gold leaf was blown away as remained on their feathers.

You can see many other Liver birds across the city: in iron or bronze, stone or timber, mosaic or glass, gilded or painted. They adorn the grandest banks, museums, and offices, as well as factories, pubs, hospitals, and cemeteries, and you don't need to be a birdwatcher to spot them.

Address Royal Liver Building, Liverpool Waterfront L3 1HU, Tel +44 1512364859 |
Getting there 5-minute walk from James Street station | Tip The giant bronze doors of
7 Water Street, formerly a bank, have lions' heads with open jaws and ferocious teeth,
which sailors used to stroke for good luck before going to sea.

61 Liverpool One Bridewell

Eat and drink in a police cell

Burgers, steaks, scouse, fish and chips, or sausage and mash, washed down with real ale or a glass of wine: the fare now served here is an improvement on the meagre rations given to the original inmates, and is brought to your table rather than being shoved through a flap in the door. A bridewell is a prison for petty offenders, named after the one in London which was near St Bride's Well. There were once ten in Liverpool: this one has been converted into a pub and restaurant.

Liverpool One Bridewell is surrounded by a blank brick wall leading to a courtyard, now filled with tables for outdoor eating; inside is the bar, and beyond it is a dark, narrow corridor with cramped cells on either side, each with a flagstone floor, brick vault, and a metal-faced door. Being banged up here must have been grim. The cells now are cosy, each one a little diner, but the convivial atmosphere cannot quite banish a few shudders. Upstairs were the police officers' quarters: they lived on-site, and unlike the cells, their rooms have large windows. This floor has been opened up to make an airy space for functions and events.

Charles Dickens came several times to Liverpool for amateur theatricals or public readings of his work. On one occasion he enrolled as a special constable for the night and toured the docklands with the superintendent of police. He was taken to disreputable houses and sailors' drinking dens, where he saw boozers and swindlers. It is sometimes claimed that he was based at Liverpool One Bridewell, but he did not mention it when he wrote about his tour of the city's underworld.

However, Liverpool One Bridewell can definitely be associated with celebrities of a different kind: Frankie Goes to Hollywood and the La's played here when, in a later phase of its chequered history, the building was used as a recording studio and rehearsal space.

Address 1 Campbell Square, Argyle Street, Liverpool L 1 5FB, Tel +44 1517097000,
www.liverpoolonebridewell.com | **Getting there** 10-minute walk from Central station;
5-minute walk from Liverpool One bus station | **Hours** Sun–Fri noon–11pm,
Sat noon–midnight | **Tip** The main bridewell, an even more grim-looking building off
Dale Street, is now a hotel.

62 Liverpool Overhead Railway

The Dockers' Umbrella

The Liverpool Overhead Railway gallery in the Museum of Liverpool evokes vivid images of the first electric elevated railway in the world, demolished more than 55 years ago and still mourned by the city's inhabitants. Here you can climb aboard an original third-class coach bound for Dingle, with hard wooden seats and "No Spitting" signs. Projected alongside are early film footage by the Lumière Brothers of an 1896 journey on the railway and a re-creation of that trip in artist Ben Parry's 2008 film *Terminus*.

Built in 1893 and running the full seven miles of docks, Liverpool Overhead Railway was also the first railway to use automatic signalling and electric coloured signal lights. Trains travelled from Seaforth Sands to Dingle with 17 intermediate stations, and for most of its length the railway followed the line of the tall dock boundary wall. There was also a dockland steam railway, and since the overhead railway's tracks ran above it in places, the track bed was plated to prevent debris falling from passing trains. This made it waterproof and earned it the nickname "Dockers' Umbrella," as it provided shelter for dock workers in wet weather. As well as being a transport system for the dockers, it was a popular leisure attraction, and visitors were fascinated to see the waterfront crowded with sailing vessels and steamships.

In 1955, a survey revealed extensive corrosion of the ironwork. The estimated cost of repairs at £2 million was beyond the means of the railway company, and the following year the structure was dismantled. Apart from the surviving carriage and other memorabilia in the museum, the only remains are iron stanchions embedded in the boundary wall at the Princes and Wapping docks and the tunnel portal at Herculaneum Dock, where the "Dockers' Umbrella" forsook the heights and burrowed underground.

Address Museum of Liverpool, Pier Head, Liverpool L 3 1DG, Tel +44 1514784545, www.liverpoolmuseums.org.uk/mol | **Getting there** 5-minute walk from James Street station | **Hours** Daily 10am–5pm, closed Dec 24 from 2pm, Dec 25–26, and Jan 1 | **Tip** Oh Me Oh My is a grand tea house with a roof garden at West Africa House (25 Water Street, Mon–Fri 9am–4pm).

63_Liverpool Resurgent

Aka Dickie Lewis

Above the main entrance to the former Lewis's department store at the corner of Ranelagh Street is a gigantic bronze by Jacob Epstein. The naked man with outstretched arms striding forward on the prow of a ship was commissioned by the store, a Liverpool institution for more than 150 years. Founded by David Lewis in 1856, it sold clothes at prices working people could afford. The business quickly prospered, boosted by stunts such as mooring the *Great Eastern*, the world's largest steamship, in the Mersey to act as a floating advertisement, and releasing a celebrated music hall song called "Lewis's Beautiful Tea." The store grew and grew, until the night of 4 May 1941, when it was flattened by a bomb.

Undaunted, Lewis's decided to rebuild. The new building was more magnificent than ever, with seven retail floors, banks of escalators, and numerous works of art. Epstein's nude figure *Liverpool Resurgent*, unveiled in 1956, was a symbol of the city's recovery from wartime destruction. Some claimed that its nudity would corrupt schoolgirls' minds, but this did not stop it becoming a landmark and a favourite meeting place for courting couples. Its huge scale makes it easy to miss three smaller sculptures of scenes from childhood, also by Epstein, immediately above the entrance doors. He admired children's spontaneity and vividly captured their carefree actions in his charming reliefs.

Sadly, Lewis's closed in 2010 and now the building is being refurbished for other uses. Some of the store's other artworks are incorporated into the public areas of the Adagio Hotel, including a stunning tiled mural depicting fruit, vegetables, pots, and pans in zingy Festival-of-Britain colours, and a set of incised wooden panels portraying the history of Liverpool. The Epstein figure still presides over the street corner and remains known locally by its cheeky nickname, Dickie Lewis.

Address Lewis's Building, Ranelagh Street, Liverpool L1 1QE | **Getting there** 2-minute walk from Central station | **Tip** A short distance up Renshaw Street is Grand Central, the former Methodist Hall and now the place to shop for punk, goth, and hippie styles.

64 Loophonium

A musical joke by a Liverpool wit

Most people go to the Walker Art Gallery to see world-famous paintings by the likes of Rembrandt and Rossetti, Holbein and Hockney, but among the serious art there is something to make you laugh. The *Loophonium* is a purposely ridiculous combination of a silver-plated euphonium joined to a toilet bowl; the wooden lavatory seat has been turned into a lyre or harp by the addition of bits of string, giving rise to its alternative title, the Harpic-chord (after the brand of toilet cleaner advertised with the once-familiar slogan, "Harpic cleans right round the bend").

The combination of music, plays on words, and lavatorial humour was typical of its creator, Fritz Spiegl, who came to the city as a 13-year-old Jewish refugee from Austria and became the principal flautist of the Royal Liverpool Philharmonic orchestra. He was a man of many parts: he rediscovered a lost opera by Donizetti called *Emilia di Liverpool*, first performed in Naples in 1824, which was later recorded by Joan Sutherland; he wrote the theme tune to the TV series *Z-Cars*; he was a nationally known broadcaster, journalist, wit, and local historian. Spiegl took to the humorous traditions of his adopted city (or in local parlance, its "sensa Yuma") and wrote a definitive guide to its unique language, *Lern Yerself Scouse*. He specialized in musical jokes, writing his *Concerto for Two Tuning Forks*, and the *Motor Horn Concerto*, performed with a vintage car onstage.

Spiegl made the *Loophonium* for an April Fools' Day concert with the Liverpool Philharmonic in 1960 (the floral decoration on the bowl was the work of his daughter Emily). He played it himself, and when the orchestra performed "God Save the Queen," he would lift the seat to show respect. You can hear the throaty tones of the *Loophonium* playing "Frère Jacques" by pressing the button next to it, or by visiting YouTube.

Address Walker Art Gallery, William Brown Street, Liverpool L3 8EL, Tel +44 1514794199, www.liverpoolmuseums.org.uk/walker | **Getting there** 3-minute walk from Lime Street station | **Hours** Daily 10am–5pm, closed Dec 24 from 2pm, Dec 25–26, and Jan 1 | **Tip** The Small Cinema (57–59 Victoria Street), in the old Magistrate's Court building, is a 60-seat volunteer-run cinema, screening a mix of mainstream and alternative films, old and new.

65 Lunya

Liverpool "meats" Catalonia

Peter Kinsella discovered Catalan cuisine while on a business trip to Barcelona. He and his wife, Elaine, now run one of the most interesting foodie destinations in the UK, dedicated to Catalonian cuisine. The exterior of their elegantly refurbished early warehouse has a sleek, black modern look, contrasting with the 18th-century brickwork: inside is a deli, bar, and spacious restaurant on two levels. The rough brick walls are enlivened with colourful modern pictures and papier-mâché sculptures.

In the brightly lit deli, giant hams hang from the ceiling above a tempting display of cheeses and cured meats. There are shelves of dry goods – paella rice, flours, spices, and striking yellow tins of Saula coffee; bottles of virgin olive oils and wines; different varieties of olives; and colourful tins of anchovies and sardines. The quality is superb; most of the produce comes from small artisan makers sourced on regular trips to Spain, with fresh foods from local suppliers. Everything is available online, including paella pans and beautiful non-folksy pottery.

Standards in the restaurant are equally high. The menu is mainly Catalan or Spanish, although Liverpool meets Barcelona in a few items, such as "full English fusion breakfast" and Lunya's signature tapas, "Catalan Scouse" – more successful than it might sound, adding chorizo and morcilla to the traditional ingredients. The tapas can be simple – a plate of wafer-thin slices of chorizo from acorn-fed pigs, or a few delicious smoked anchovies – but some are more complex, such as slow-cooked chicken "al moro" in cumin and saffron sauce, with preserved lemon. Paellas are made to order and cheese is served with membrillo or other sweetmeats. Classic desserts include "Crema Catalana," topped with crunchy caramel. Lunya also holds regular gourmet evenings, suckling pig banquets, and master classes in ham carving.

Address 18–21 College Lane, Liverpool L1 3DS, Tel +44 1517069770, www.lunya.co.uk |
Getting there 5-minute walk from Central station | **Hours** Mon–Tue 10am–9pm,
Wed–Thu 10am–9:30pm, Fri 10am–10pm, Sat 9am–10:30pm, Sun 10am–8:30pm |
Tip Watch the theatrical performance in the window of Barber Barber next door, where
gentlemen's haircuts, cut-throat shaving with hot towels, and beard-sculpting are all
part of the show.

66__Maray

The world's first falafel and cocktail restaurant

Maray is an informal restaurant serving cocktails and Middle Eastern-influenced food with a seasonally changing menu of small and big plates. It was started by three friends, Dom and John, who had ambitions of opening a cocktail bar; and James, a foodie with a yen for falafel. During a weekend in Paris, they visited Le Marais, the historic central district full of bars, and also home to the famous L'As du Fallafel, a mecca for enthusiasts of the Middle Eastern deep-fried chickpea balls. Returning to Liverpool, they decided to combine their interests, and the result was Maray – so spelled because they didn't want to be mistaken for a French restaurant.

Maray is more sophisticated than its Parisian inspiration. While falafel is typically a fast food, Maray is a place to linger, and to savour subtle combinations that are adventurous without being wilful. The cocktails are inventive – try a beetroot and hibiscus G&T or a margarita with blood oranges and you'll be pleasantly surprised at first sip.

The food is equally interesting. In the brief asparagus season, they serve local asparagus from Claremont Farm on the Wirral with rhubarb, fried duck egg, and hazelnuts. Claremont also supplies courgette flowers which are sometimes stuffed with whipped goat cheese and combined with watercress and pickled radish. Figs come with local honey. Big plates include vegetarian dishes as well as meat or fish. The falafel has just the right combination of crunchiness and herby softness. The lunch menu includes a falafel sandwich with Maray's homemade delicious green tahini, in a wrap that is a million miles above the usual cardboard flatbread.

The decor is industrial chic, with exposed brick walls, sewing-machine tables, French school chairs, and a long communal table that runs down the centre, exemplifying the sharing philosophy behind this enterprising eatery.

Address 91 Bold Street, Liverpool L1 4HF, Tel +44 1517095820 www.maray.co.uk | **Getting there** 5-minute walk from Central station | **Hours** Mon–Thu noon–10pm, Fri–Sat noon–11pm, Sun noon–9pm | **Tip** Matta's International Foods (51 Bold Street) has a huge selection of spices, herbs, pulses, noodles, sauces, and fresh fruit and vegetables for every type of cuisine.

67 __Mathew Street on Saturday Night

Where Liverpool comes out to play

During the day, Mathew Street is a honeytrap for Beatles tourists, thronging outside the Cavern Club, which isn't really the Cavern Club at all (that was demolished in 1973), and the Cavern Pub, which wasn't even there in the 1960s. They take selfies with the shiny statue of John Lennon. They stare at the sculpture of Carl Jung, who wrote, "Liverpool is the pool of life." They inspect the Liverpool Wall of Fame, with its 17 Beatles chart-toppers as well as "How Much Is That Doggie in the Window?" by Lita Roza (number one in 1953).

Mathew Street at night is something else entirely. Go there around 11:30pm on a Friday or Saturday, and like an anthropologist in the jungle, you will find yourself in another world, surrounded by alien species. These are not tourists but Liverpool's finest, out for a night on the tiles. Taxis at the end of the street disgorge the crowds: teenage girls dolled up to the nines, tottering on high heels – glitter clutch-bag in one hand, cigarette in the other – wearing pelmet skirts and strapless tops exposing bare shoulders (and more). The young men wear a more sober uniform comprising a tight short-sleeved shirt hanging out of dark trousers or skinny jeans, trainers, and hair in a buzz-cut or extravagantly brushed up. Coats are rarely worn by either sex, even in midwinter.

Hen parties heave into sight: more teetering stilettos, but now all the girls are identically clad in fancy dress (nurse, sailor, ballerina, or cowgirl) or frilly skirts and bunny ears, fairy wings, and pink satin sashes printed with the name of the bride or birthday girl. The decibel rate is high: throbbing music issues forth from bars, and whoops and screams issue forth from revellers, all in richly nasal Scouse. It's all good fun: the atmosphere is friendly, good-humoured, and entertaining, and there is a discreet police presence, just in case.

68__Museum of Dentistry

Teeth, tiles, and Tate

This macabre display will either make you feel thankful for modern dentistry or put you off going to the dentist altogether. It includes alarming-looking instruments used for extractions and horrid metal contraptions that were clamped round the face to ensure that dentures had the correct bite, as well as numerous different types of teeth, real and artificial. You can also peer into a re-created dentist's surgery, with a Victorian dentist's chair and a Heath Robinson-style 1920s X-ray machine.

There are ivory dentures, porcelain dentures (the material was supplied by Wedgwood), and teeth that were held in with springs, designed to stop them falling out when you opened your mouth (not always successful). Even more disconcerting are the dentures made from human teeth, taken from the corpses of soldiers killed in battle: as the soldiers were young and healthy, their teeth were in better condition than those obtained from paupers or grave robbers. After 1815, dentures made from real teeth became known as "Waterloo teeth" because so many came from the battlefield of Waterloo.

The Museum of Dentistry dates back to 1880, when it was started by the precursor to today's University of Liverpool School of Dentistry. In 2008, it was relocated to the beautifully restored Victoria Building, designed by Liverpool architect Alfred Waterhouse. The intensely red colour of the brick and terracotta gave rise to the term "red brick university." Inside is a double-height entrance hall, lined with tiles and now housing a stylish cafe, popular with university staff. There is an art gallery on the first floor and the dentistry collection is displayed on the second floor in the Tate Hall, formerly the University Library: ironically, considering the connection between sugar and tooth decay, the Hall was funded by Sir Henry Tate, the sugar refiner.

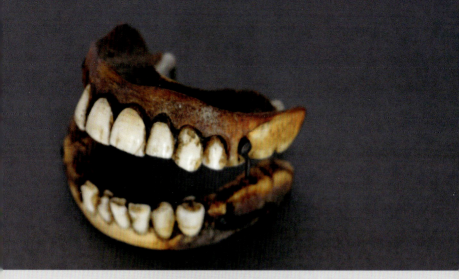

Address Victoria Gallery and Museum, Ashton Street, Liverpool L 69 3DR (Sat Nav L 3 5TR), Tel +44 1517942348, www.vgm.liverpool.ac.uk | **Getting there** 15-minute walk from Lime Street station; CityLink bus from Liverpool One bus station or bus 79 from Queen Square bus station, both to top of Brownlow Hill | **Hours** Tue – Sat 10am – 5pm; Cafe: Mon – Fri 9am – 4pm, Sat 11am – 2pm | **Tip** Cross the main road, turn left and go under the bridge; a few minutes' walk will take you to Barbara Hepworth's bronze sculpture *Squares with Two Circles*.

69__ The Music Room
New vibes at the Phil

The Royal Liverpool Philharmonic may be the UK's oldest professional symphony orchestra, with a proud history of music making, but it is not resting on its laurels. A new performance venue has opened at the Phil, designed by Caruso St John Architects, with a lively line-up of roots, folk, jazz, new, and world music, as well as classical ensembles from the orchestra's talented players. The Music Room is a flexible space, the style is informal, and seating is cabaret-style – or even standing. There are lunchtime concerts, daytime rehearsals, master classes, and evening gigs. A bar serves refreshments during concerts and events, and on most days you'll find there is something interesting going on.

The Music Room is the last piece in a series of major renovations to the celebrated Art Deco concert hall, designed in the 1930s by Herbert J. Rowse. The first phase included improvements to the auditorium and the stylish public areas. The entrance foyer, which had been altered, has now been returned to its original layout, and the grand foyer at first-floor level has a new island bar which is open during the day. These elegant spaces have been redecorated in their Deco-era colour schemes.

Rowse, who was also the architect for the Mersey Tunnel and India Buildings, always worked closely with a trusted team of artists. At the Phil, the artist Hector Whistler etched images of musical instruments into the glass entrance doors and large first-floor windows overlooking Hope Street. Just inside is a memorial to the musicians of the *Titanic*, several of whom were from Liverpool. The glittering gilded reliefs of Orpheus charming the wild beasts with his music on each side of the grand foyer are the work of Edmund C. Thompson. Both art and music have a long and enthusiastic following in the city, and the Phil styles itself as the "original Liverpool sound."

Address Liverpool Philharmonic Hall, Hope Street, Liverpool L1 9BP, Tel +44 1517093789, www.liverpoolphil.com | **Getting there** 12-minute walk from Central station; CityLink bus from Liverpool One bus station to Hope Street | **Tip** The Quarter (10 Falkner Street), a family-run deli and cafe/restaurant, is a 2-minute walk from the Phil and stays open after concerts (Mon–Fri 8am–11pm, Sat and Sun 9am–11pm).

70__National Wildflower Centre

A haven for bumblebees

From a walled garden in Knowsley, the charity Landlife is planning a countrywide network of urban wildflower meadows and community green spaces. The National Wildflower Centre is a showcase for this beautiful cause. Court Hey Park, where the centre is located, was the home of Robert Gladstone, elder brother of the Prime Minister William Gladstone. The house fell into disrepair after World War II and was demolished, but the grounds became a public park. In 2000 Landlife took over the stables and erected a long, narrow concrete-and-glass building between the walled garden and the park. It comes as a surprise to find that the flat roof is planted as a wildflower meadow with views over the vibrant gardens below.

The displays feature more than 400 British wildflowers. Many have medicinal purposes, and are loved by birds and insects. Visitors are attracted by viper's bugloss, once believed to heal snakebites, and by fox and cubs, an orange hawkweed native to the Alps. In spring there are snake's head fritillaries with their purple chequered bell-shaped flowers. Evening primroses open their bright yellow petals at dusk to attract nocturnal insects. Teasels are tall, stately plants with prickly seed heads, which are still used to comb the felt on billiard tables. You can buy seeds for these and many other wildflowers in the centre's shop. There is also the friendly Cornflower Cafe, with a good range of homemade soups and cakes.

While the demonstration areas show how wildflower habitats can be planted and managed, Landlife's main activity is working with communities across Britain to encourage creative conservation. Their biggest scheme, called A Tale of Two Cities, involves Liverpool and Manchester, where large drifts of wildflowers are being planted in prominent public places to establish colourful havens for wildlife.

Address Court Hey Park, Roby Road, Liverpool L 16 3NA, Tel +44 1517381913, www.nwc.org.uk | **Getting there** Train to Broadgreen station, then a 10-minute walk; bus 79 or 79D from Liverpool One station to Chelwood Avenue; bus 6 or 61 from Queen Square station to Roby Road | **Hours** Apr 1–Sept 30, Mon–Sun 10am–5pm; Oct 1–Mar 31, only the cafe is open, Mon–Fri 10am–4pm | **Tip** A 15-minute walk south of Court Hey Park is All Saints Childwall (Childwall Abbey Road), the only remaining medieval church in Liverpool, with a fine interior (for opening hours call Tel +44 1515385973).

71__ The Nelson Monument

A hero for Liverpool traders

The square known as Exchange Flags was once the beating heart of commercial Liverpool, buzzing with cotton merchants and brokers exchanging news and cutting deals. They preferred to do business in the open air. At first they traded in the old Exchange, an arcaded courtyard within the Town Hall; small and dark, it was soon filled in by the present grand staircase. The area outside was then paved to make a new space for trading and surrounded by elegant classical buildings, with an open arcade at ground level (completed 1808). In the centre a magnificent monument to the great naval commander Horatio Nelson was erected (1813), the work of the sculptors Matthew Cotes Wyatt and Richard Westmacott.

By 1870, the square had been rebuilt in a more grandiose manner, but soon afterwards trading was transformed by the invention of the telegraph and the telephone. The merchants retreated indoors and the character of the square changed. In 1906 a purpose-built Cotton Exchange was opened nearby in Old Hall Street. The square was remodelled yet again between 1939 and 1955, with the bland buildings that you see today. Later an underground car park was constructed, and the monument had to be raised onto a new podium. The four dramatic bronze statues of chained captives (not slaves as is sometimes thought) represent Nelson's main victories, also pictured in relief panels. At the top is Nelson, an idealised nude being crowned as the victor of Trafalgar (1805) even as a skeleton reaches out to claim him (he died in the battle). A strategically positioned flag conceals his missing arm.

You might not think that Nelson was particularly relevant to the cotton trade, but he was: the monument is here not only to commemorate his heroism but because his victories enabled Liverpool ships to continue sailing the seas and trading freely, thus safeguarding the city's prosperity.

Address Exchange Flags, Liverpool L2 3YL | **Getting there** 3-minute walk from James Street station | **Tip** Moose Coffee (6 Dale Street) serves American- and Canadian-style breakfast and brunch dishes, pancakes, and deli sandwiches. Try their "New York Moose" (eggs Benedict), hash browns, or waffles with maple syrup.

72__News from Nowhere

Bookshop run by the real Amazons

From its rainbow flag, red-painted shop front and the placards in its window, the radical credentials of News from Nowhere are clear. Inside are posters for sundry left-wing causes and community organisations, and a rack of anarchist and socialist magazines. The shop has the slightly shabby air of a students' union, but it has proved itself by its staying power. Founded in 1974, News from Nowhere is the oldest established bookshop in Liverpool, and one of a dying breed of alternative bookshops in the UK. It has defied market trends: "Think Global, Shop Local" and "Buy from the real Amazons" are its slogans.

Its response to the decline of independent bookshops was to start its own online store. News from Nowhere is not, however, a conventional business. It is a not-for-profit organisation run by a women's co-operative of five or six members. All tasks and decisions are shared, all members are paid equally, and all profits go back into overhead costs or book stock.

The range of literary subjects is enormous: feminism, gender, sexuality, health and well-being, spirituality, political activism, anti-racism, anti-capitalism, civil rights, disability rights, parenting, sustainability, and ethical living. On the lighter side, there are also world music CDs, a selection of current fiction, and children's books, but with an emphasis on diversity and social issues. It makes for a great place to browse and discover, and the specialist knowledge of the staff is impressive.

How has it survived? Rents in Bold Street continue to rise, but News from Nowhere can to a certain extent avoid commercial pressures because it owns its building, purchased with donations from supporters. The shop takes its name from William Morris's utopian novel about a future of social justice, equality, and common ownership; Morris would most definitely have approved.

Address 96 Bold Street, Liverpool L1 4HY, Tel +44 1517087270, www.newsfromnowhere.org.uk | **Getting there** 5-minute walk from Central station | **Hours** Mon–Sat 10am–5:45pm, most Sun 11am–5pm | **Tip** Liverpool's radical history is depicted in the painting *Unemployment on Merseyside: Campaigning for the Right to Work* by Mike Jones, on show at the Museum of Liverpool (Liverpool Waterfront, Pier Head).

73__Old Dock

Where it all began

Far below the fashion shops of Liverpool One is the Old Dock, which catapulted Liverpool from a small backwater town into a global mercantile hub. Built in 1715, it was the world's first commercial enclosed wet dock, and it had a huge impact on trade. Before this, ships had to moor in the Pool, a tidal inlet that gave Liverpool its name, and which became a muddy expanse at low tide. The dock was an expensive and risky venture, but by allowing ships to load and unload at all states of the tide, it slashed the time needed from two weeks to two and a half days.

The experimental structure, designed by canal engineer Thomas Steers, was built at the mouth of the Pool, with walls of brick laid on bedrock and a gate that opened from the river. Around the wet dock were quays onto which goods were unloaded. Originally the Old Dock accommodated 100 vessels, but as the size of ships increased, it became too small, and other docks took its place. In 1826 it was closed and used as the site for a huge custom house that in turn was demolished after sustaining bomb damage in World War II. Yet the original walls of the dock remained underground and were rediscovered during the construction of Liverpool One.

You can see a section of the original wall by peering through a circular window in the paving outside John Lewis; but much more revealing is a free guided tour starting at the Maritime Museum. It takes you down to the original quayside, 40 feet below ground level, where a large expanse of the wall is exposed and the operation of the dock can be understood. The tour guides, who are entertaining as well as informative, also include the story behind the fountain that runs from Liverpool One to the Albert Dock. This celebrates William Hutchinson, master of the Old Dock, who pioneered the science of tidal movements and their prediction as an aid to navigation.

Address Thomas Steers Way, Liverpool L1 8LW | **Getting there** 2-minute walk from Liverpool One bus station; 8-minute walk from James Street station | **Hours** Tours are on Tue and Wed at 10:30am, 11:30am, and 2:30pm, and start from Maritime Museum, Albert Dock L3 4AQ; booking ahead is essential: Tel +44 1514784499, www.liverpoolmuseums.org.uk/maritime | **Tip** The Open Eye Gallery (19 Mann Island), alongside the Museum of Liverpool, has an international programme of cutting-edge contemporary photography (Tue–Sun 10:30am–5:30pm during exhibitions).

74_ Old Hebrew Synagogue

A masterpiece of opulent Orientalism

Princes Road was laid out beginning in the 1840s with a series of eye-catching palaces of worship, the most lavish of which is the Old Hebrew Synagogue. With the exodus of Liverpool's merchant class to the suburbs, the city-centre synagogue was no longer convenient. An architectural competition for its replacement was won in 1871 by the Scottish architects W & G Audsley, who had already built the Welsh Presbyterian Church, with its audacious spire, on the other side of Princes Road. The synagogue is in an eclectic style with a Gothic rose window and a Moorish-style horseshoe arch over the portal; originally it had minarets on top of the turrets.

In contrast to the monochrome exterior of red brick, red sandstone, and polished red granite, the interior is a breathtaking Aladdin's cave of colour and pattern. Every surface is stencilled or gilded with floral and abstract patterns shimmering on a mint green background; the lines of the arcades and the soaring vault are painted in red, green, and gold.

The seats in the aisles and galleries – men below and women above – face inwards, towards the marble and alabaster *bimah* (reading platform) in the centre, lit by candelabra. Here, portions of the Torah are read out each week at Sabbath morning service. At the west is an ornate pulpit, and behind it is the ark, where the scrolls of the Torah are kept. This is the climax of the interior, a gilded fantasy of Gothic, Assyrian, and Grecian motifs, surmounted by brilliant blue domes decorated with stars and Hebrew inscriptions. Behind is a rose window with jewel-like stained glass.

Once threatened with closure as the Jewish community moved on to the outer suburbs, the synagogue has been restored and is now enjoying a revival. In the words of a Jewish historian, "He who has not seen the interior of Princes Road synagogue in Liverpool has not beheld the glory of Israel."

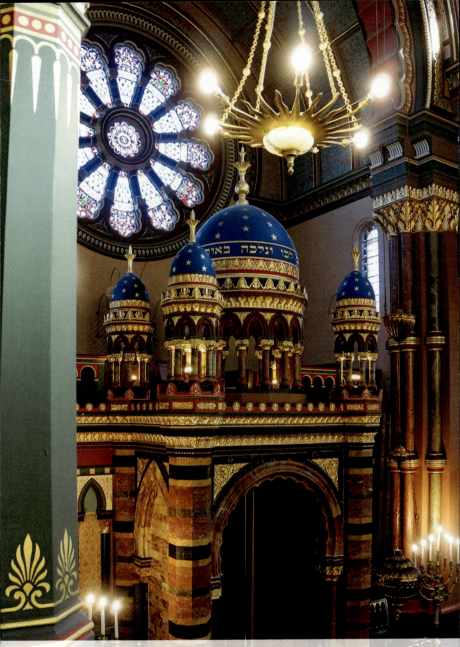

Address Liverpool Old Hebrew Congregation, Synagogue Chambers, Princes Road, Liverpool L 8 1TG, Tel +44 1517093431, www.princesroad.org, tours@princesroad.org | **Getting there** Bus 75, 86, or 86A from Liverpool One bus station to Huskisson Street | **Hours** Guided tours Mon–Thu 9:30am–3:30pm; booking essential | **Tip** In Berkley Street is the magnificent Greek Orthodox Church of St Nicholas, built in 1870. It is open for Sunday mass from 10am and on Monday morning during cleaning (Tel +44 1517099543).

75 __ Olwen's Staircase

Art gallery with a unique attachment

Olwen McLaughlin's Editions gallery at 16 Cook Street always has lively exhibitions by North West artists. But what makes each visit a special pleasure is to see inside one of Liverpool's most extraordinary buildings. It is difficult to believe that it dates from 1864 to 1866, for the first-floor gallery is reached via a spiral cast-iron staircase, cantilevered out from the rear of the building and wrapped in a glass tube. Technically and architecturally far ahead of its time, this staircase provides a thrilling ascent.

No. 16 Cook Street was designed by the Liverpool architect and surveyor Peter Ellis to maximise daylight, with tall window bays at the front and curtain walling at the rear, divided into horizontal bands. To make the building fireproof, the columns are cast iron and the floors are vaulted in brick. It is one of only two buildings by Ellis to survive. The other is the nearby Oriel Chambers in Water Street, scorned in its day as "an agglomeration of protruding glass bubbles," but now celebrated as a proto-modernist masterpiece. Completed in 1864, its street façades consist of rows of oriel windows hiding the structure behind with the slenderest of frames so as to maximise the area of glass.

Ellis's work is thought to have influenced the Chicago architect John Welborn Root, one of the pioneers of the skyscraper. Root studied in Liverpool from 1864 to 1867 before returning to America, and would certainly have seen the two buildings. In later life Ellis became an inventor, patenting an improved form of water closet, a set of exploding firearms, and a device to prevent fraud among omnibus conductors. His most remarkable invention was the world's first paternoster lift, which was installed in Oriel Chambers in 1869. Although Ellis never became a Liverpool celebrity in his lifetime, Olwen is, and she will give you a friendly welcome at her gallery.

Address Editions, 16 Cook Street, Liverpool L2 9RG, Tel +44 0512364236, www.editionsltd.net | **Getting there** 5-minute walk from James Street station | **Hours** Mon–Fri 9:30am–5:30pm, Sat 11am–4pm | **Tip** Another spectacular staircase, designed by Eva Jiricna in steel and glass, can be seen inside Boodle's Jewellery Shop (Mon–Sat 9:30am–5:30pm) on the corner of Lord and North John streets.

76__Opera for Chinatown

The forgotten histories of the Liverpool Chinese

The oldest Chinese community in Europe can be found in Liverpool, although Liverpool's Chinatown is probably the smallest in the world. Its centre is Berry Street, where in 2000, a Chinese arch was built by craftsmen from Shanghai, now twinned with Liverpool. It is the largest arch outside China. In 2014, in nearby Duke Street, the Sound Agents, an artist-run organisation with an interest in revealing hidden social history, created another sizeable artwork, *Opera for Chinatown*, which celebrates the cultural heritage of Liverpool's Chinese population.

In the mid-Victorian period, Liverpool ships dominated the trade between Britain and China. The Blue Funnel Line, owned by Alfred Holt of Liverpool, employed many Chinese seamen, and some settled in Liverpool, opening shops, restaurants, and laundries, and marrying local girls. Chinese seamen also served in the British merchant fleet in both World Wars. In the 1940s, the British recruited thousands of Chinese seamen and based them in Liverpool. Many lost their lives in the Battle of the Atlantic, but after the war, those remaining were no longer wanted, and many were forcibly repatriated. In 2006, a memorial plaque was unveiled on the Pier Head honouring the exiled Chinese seamen and those who had died fighting for Britain.

In a happier episode, Chinese children from Liverpool were chosen to act as extras alongside Ingrid Bergman in the movie *The Inn of the Sixth Happiness*, based on the story of Gladys Aylward, the British missionary to China.

Opera for Chinatown is like a performance in three acts, a visual archive of the Blue Funnel sailors, the repatriation, and the Bergman film. In the windows of three Duke Street houses awaiting renovation is a montage of photographs, passports, identity cards, and Blue Funnel Line posters, with a portrait of Grace Liu, a famous Cantonese opera singer, in the centre.

DUKE ST.
公爵街

Address 151–155 Duke Street, Liverpool L 1 4JR | **Getting there** 7-minute walk from Central station | **Tip** The Pagoda Youth Orchestra, based at Pagoda Arts in Henry Street, is the first and largest Chinese Youth Orchestra in Europe. If you get the opportunity to see them, they will amaze you.

77__Outhouse

More than just a glass box

Set amongst trees planted between mundane tower blocks near Woolton is a small glass box with no obvious purpose. The door is usually locked, but you can see right into it. There are bits and pieces inside – posters, display panels, art materials, chairs – left over from various activities, as well as mysterious stone blocks. This is *Outhouse*, an intriguing public art piece designed by husband and wife Vong Phaophanit and Claire Oboussier.

Phaophanit achieved brief fame in 1993, when he filled a gallery at the Tate in London with mounds of rice covering neon lights, combining modern technology with memories of his upbringing in Laos. The origins of *Outhouse* are very different. In the 1980s, the government set up Housing Action Trusts to improve poor-quality council housing estates. The Liverpool HAT was the largest, with 5,332 properties in 67 tower blocks. It was given 12 years and £260 million of government money. After consulting with tenants it decided to demolish 54 of the blocks and build new houses on the land, while refurbishing the other towers. Unusually, the Liverpool HAT decided to use the power of art to engage residents and commissioned *Outhouse*. Its design is a reduced version of the new terraced houses built nearby: like them, it has a sloping roof and a door at one side. But unlike them, *Outhouse*'s walls are completely transparent, while interior doorways are represented by stone blocks.

Since it was completed in 2005, *Outhouse* has been animated at night with projected images; it has been used to display poppies on Remembrance Sunday, and it has housed musical events and art workshops. Even when it stands empty, the glass walls reflect the surrounding vegetation and refract the light into delicate patterns, so that the structure changes its appearance at different times of day and throughout the seasons.

Address Menlove Avenue, Woolton, Liverpool L25 6ET | **Getting there** Bus 76 from Liverpool One bus station to Menlove Avenue Limecroft/Evesham Close | **Tip** Woolton Picture House in Woolton Village (3 Mason Street), the only single-screen cinema left in Liverpool, retains many of its Art Deco features and still has intervals with usherettes selling ice cream.

78__Panoramic 34
Sky-high bar and restaurant

Panoramic 34 is the highest restaurant in the UK outside London and the views are simply stunning: the restaurant looks over the Mersey, which is wider than the Thames, so that from this height the river and cityscape are even more majestic than in London. Views on the north side extend from the docks to Liverpool Bay and Blackpool; those to the south include the Liver Building and upriver; the west-facing tables look right down on the Mersey and across to the Wirral. Cruise liners moor just below, and you can watch the ferries and other river traffic come and go. This is the very best place in the city to get your bearings.

As the name indicates, the restaurant is on the 34th floor of West Tower, one of the new "scousescrapers" in the shiny new central business district. The interior is redolent of 1980s luxury, fitted with dark timber-ribbed panelling and mirrors; the tables are formally laid for lunch and dinner with white tablecloths, and the bar offers comfortable leather seats. Full-height windows run around the edge, so that wherever you are, you have a splendid view.

The spectacular vistas make it difficult to concentrate on your food. Typical starters are rabbit ballantine or scallops, while main courses might include cannon of lamb, roast pheasant, or sea bass. Portions are generous, and if you are feeling adventurous, you can try dishes that include blue cheese foam or frozen rosemary cream. The chocolate lover's plate for two makes a terrific dessert. Another option is the luxury afternoon tea, with a glass of wine included.

You can also eat at the bar, or sip a cocktail, a relaxing thing to do as the sun goes down and the city gradually lights up. Although the food is good, it has a hard job, matching the quality of the views. Just make sure you don't suffer from vertigo before you give it a try.

Address West Tower, Brook Street, Liverpool L3 9PJ, Tel +44 1512365534, www.panoramic34.com | **Getting there** 5-minute walk from Moorfields station | **Hours** Bar: Tue–Sat 11am–11:30pm, Sun 11am–11pm; Restaurant: Tue–Fri noon–3pm and 6pm–9:30pm, Sat noon–2:30pm and 6pm–9:30pm, Sun noon–8pm; booking essential; smart dress code | **Tip** Ben Johnson's 2008 panorama, *The Liverpool Cityscape*, is on view in the Museum of Liverpool (Liverpool Waterfront, Pier Head).

79__Penelope
It's all unravelling

Wolstenhome Square is a mess of grungy sheds and semi-derelict buildings in the RopeWalks area, so named because it was where ropes were made for the shipping industry. Towering over the square is a strange construction of huge brightly coloured spheres attached to a network of writhing stalks, like a cluster of sci-fi antennae or gigantic spaghetti. The artwork's title, *Penelope*, refers to an episode in Homer's *Odyssey*. While Odysseus was away on his epic journey, his wife, Penelope, was besieged by suitors. To put them off, she told them she would decide which one to marry when she had finished weaving a shroud for her father-in-law, but every night she frantically unravelled the threads she had woven by day. When Odysseus returned, he killed all the suitors.

Wolstenholme Square was the first of Liverpool's squares to have a garden in the centre. Later, during the Victorian era, the surrounding buildings were used as workshops and warehouses. The square was almost destroyed in the blitz, although two Georgian houses have managed to cling to one corner. Trees were planted in 2001 in an attempt to recall the square's more elegant Georgian heyday. More recently, the area has become a clubber's paradise: the superclub Cream, now an international brand, started here, as did the Kasimier, a smaller, more arty music venue. Though a spectacular sight by day, *Penelope* comes into its own at night, when the coloured spheres light up and the square swarms with crowds of pleasure-seeking revellers.

Penelope is the work of Cuban-born Los Angeles-based artist Jorge Pardo, whose installations cross the boundaries between art, design, and architecture. Although no two of his works are alike, he often uses hanging lamps en masse to transform spaces into magical environments. There are plans to rebuild Wolstenholme Square, but *Penelope* will continue to cast her spell.

Address Wolstenholme Square, Liverpool L1 4JJ | Getting there 10-minute walk from Central station | Tip Liverpool's first public library opened near here in 1852 in the building on the corner of Duke and Slater streets, originally the Union News Room, a club where members could go and read the latest newspapers and magazines.

80__Peter Kavanagh's

Charming pub with eccentric collection of curios

Walk into Peter Kavanagh's and you might think you've strayed into Dickens' *The Old Curiosity Shop*. As you stand at the bar, you are distracted by the bizarre bric-a-brac all round you: the jars and kettles, the carved figures, the elephants, and the witch astride her broomstick. In one room, chamber pots dangle from the ceiling, in another are violins and trumpets. There are old bicycles, a flayed crocodile, a collection of old wireless sets, a gas mask. The woodwork is alive with grotesque faces. This place must be a nightmare to clean.

There are two snugs, each with murals: the "Dickens" room, with paintings inspired by *The Pickwick Papers*, and the "Hogarth" room, with scenes of serving wenches and bewigged drinkers in an "olde-worlde" tavern. They are the work of Scottish artist Eric Robertson, who, after his marriage failed, settled in Liverpool (he painted a fine view of the Cathedral, now in the Museum of Liverpool). There is a pub legend that he painted the murals to pay his drinking debts, but the reality is more prosaic: the decor was commissioned by Peter Kavanagh when he refitted the pub in 1929.

Kavanagh obtained the licence in 1897 and held it for 53 years, making him one of the longest-serving licensees in Britain. He patented a number of inventions, among them the tables incorporating built-in ashtrays with removable grilles, and cups to hold lighted pipes or cigars. The pub was called the Grapes for many years, but as locals had long known it as Peter Kavanagh's, it was renamed in his honour in 1978. The present landlady is the friendly Rita Smith, who has looked after the pub for many years (although not as long as Kavanagh). There is food at lunchtime, and there are live music nights with traditional jazz and swing, which appeal to the older clientele who are regulars. Now, will it be a Guinness or one of the local guest beers?

Address 2–6 Egerton Street, Liverpool L 8 7LY, Tel +44 15170943443 | **Getting there** Bus 75, 80, 80A, 86, or 86A from Liverpool One bus station to Huskisson Street | **Hours** Sun–Thu noon–midnight, Fri–Sat noon–1am | **Tip** Set in the wall of a former nurses' home a short walk away, on the corner of Princes Road and Upper Parliament Street, is a memorial to Florence Nightingale, showing her tending the wounded.

81 Philharmonic Dining Rooms

Liverpool's artistic pub

The Philharmonic is one of the most splendid drinking palaces in the country, famous for its riotous combination of mosaic, mahogany, and metalwork – and for the red marbleised urinals and washbasins in the sumptuous gents' toilets, a magnet for visitors of both sexes (there used to be a notice requesting ladies not to enter without permission, to ensure the privacy of the men relieving themselves.)

Designed around 1900 by the architect Walter Thomas for the Liverpool brewer Robert Cain, the building represents a collaboration of the demon drink with the muses: the decorations are by staff and students of the Liverpool School of Architecture and Applied Art, and the theme of music runs through the pub's interior – a nod to the concert hall across the road (the Victorian predecessor of the present Philharmonic Hall). However, the names of the two rooms off the main bar (Brahms and Liszt, cockney rhyming slang for pissed) are modern: when the pub opened they were the News Room and the Smoke Room.

Music is enshrined in the Brahms room with a stained-glass window of St Cecilia and the words "Music is the Universal Language of Mankind." Around the room are beaten copper panels showing singers and musicians. In the Grande Lounge, once the Billiard Room there are more copper reliefs – animals, birds, fish, and seascapes, but again music dominates: on the frieze are plaster reliefs including *The Murmur of the Sea*, a boy sitting in a shell, with semi-nude women and mermaids on either side, representing vocal music, and *Apollo with Female Attendants*, two Grecian ladies crowning a bust of the Greek god, representing instrumental music. The plasterwork is by the sculptor C. J. Allen, who later made the statue of Queen Victoria at the end of Castle Street, and the metal panels are by H. Bloomfield Bare, also responsible for the exuberant Art Nouveau entrance gates.

Address 36 Hope Street, Liverpool L1 9BX, Tel +44 1517072837 | **Getting there** 12-minute walk from Central station | **Hours** Daily 11am–midnight | **Tip** Also worth a visit is the Vines, a highly decorated pub with a predominantly Irish clientele housed in a building also designed by Walter Thomas, on the corner of Lime Street and Copperas Hill.

82 Port of Liverpool Building

For those that do business in great waters

The trio of grand buildings on the riverfront, affectionately known as the "Three Graces," is a vivid reminder of Liverpool's global importance in the early 20th century. Each is decorated with symbols of maritime and mercantile glories. All three are worth examining from the outside, but with the Port of Liverpool Building you can look inside to experience even more of its splendour.

Built in 1907 as head office of the Mersey Docks and Harbour Board, it has three entrances, a central one facing the river and two others at the rear corners. On the elaborate gate piers at the main entrance are bronze dolphins supporting globes, and at the steps you are greeted by two giant female figures in classical drapery representing Commerce and Industry. Commerce rests her arm on a sailing ship, while Industry has a cotton spindle and a loom, symbols of the port and the industrial goods that passed through it.

Once inside, a wide corridor paved in coloured marbles leads you to the octagonal hall, which soars up to the central dome with tiers of galleries at every level. These are connected by a curved staircase of grey granite from the board's own quarries in Scotland. The lift doors are encrusted with sea horses and anchors, and the windows of the hall and corridors are filled with stained glass depicting the coats of arms of the colonies and dominions of the British Empire.

Running around the base of the dome in large letters are the poetic words of Psalm 107: "They that go down to the Sea in Ships, that do business in great waters; These see the Works of the Lord, and his wonders in the deep." The harbour board adopted this as its motto, such was the supreme confidence of the merchants and shipowners who were entrusted with the imperial ambitions of the nation.

Address Pier Head, Liverpool L3 1BY | **Getting there** 5-minute walk from James Street station | **Hours** Open to the public during office hours | **Tip** Alongside is the Cunard Building, the last of the Three Graces to be built. There are plans for it to house Britain's Museum of Popular Music.

83__ The Portrait Wall

The Everyman for everyone

The Liverpool Everyman reopened in 2014 with a beautiful new theatre that won the RIBA Stirling prize for the best new building of the year. The theatre has been transformed with up-to-date technical facilities and increased space, and at the same time has retained the informal, welcoming atmosphere of the old Everyman. The generous foyers overlooking Hope Street are especially pleasant and are open all day, so even if you are not going to a play, it is a good place to visit: the street-level cafe is open from breakfast onwards, the basement bistro is open afternoons and evenings, and there are occasional tours behind the scenes.

The building's façade along Hope Street is made of glass and faces south-west. The need to shade the interior from the glaring sunlight prompted the new building's most inspired feature, the portrait wall. The idea was suggested by the Everyman's unique position between two great cathedrals. The rows of sculptured figures on the fronts of medieval cathedrals often represent kings and saints, and sometimes artisans and peasants; the Everyman's exterior is a modern equivalent, proud of its diversity and inclusivity. Liverpudlians of all ages and backgrounds were invited to have their pictures taken by local photographer Dan Kenyon. He took more than 4,000, from which 105 were selected. Each figure was enlarged to life size, cut out of an aluminium plate using pioneering water-jet technology, and made into a swivelling shutter.

As these vertical louvres are moved during the day, they catch the sunlight at varying angles; inside, they cast intriguing shadows, and they look different again by night when the foyer is lit up inside. The Everyman has always taken its commitment to its local audience more seriously than most other regional theatres; to represent this commitment physically in the fabric of the theatre was a stroke of genius.

Address 5–11 Hope Street, Liverpool L1 9BH, Tel +44 1517094776, www.everymanplayhouse.com | **Getting there** 12-minute walk from Central station; CityLink bus from Liverpool One bus station to Hope Street | **Hours** Cafe: Mon–Thu 8:30am–11pm, Fri & Sat 8:30am–midnight, Sun 10am-3pm; Bistro: Mon–Sat noon–3pm, 5pm–10pm | **Tip** Try Liverpool Gin at the Belvedere (5 Sugnall Street, off Falkner Street), the tiny pub where the gin was created.

84 The Pyramid

Monument to a forgotten railway engineer

Among the neglected headstones and obelisks in the burial ground next to St Andrew's Scottish Presbyterian Church in Rodney Street stands a granite pyramid 15 feet tall. In the 1820s, when the Grecian-style church by the architect John Foster was built, this was a fashionable residential area. The attractive Georgian houses are now mainly medical consulting rooms, and St Andrew's, damaged by fire in the 1980s, has been converted into student housing.

The pyramid marks the grave of William Mackenzie. His fame has been eclipsed by that of his better-known contemporaries Thomas Telford and Isambard Kingdom Brunel. Mackenzie started out as an engineer of canals and bridges, but made a fortune as a railway contractor. His success with the tunnel works between Lime Street and Edge Hill on the Liverpool and Manchester Railway led to his taking on contracts to build railways not just all over England and Scotland but throughout Europe. After building the Paris-to-Rouen railway, he and his partner, Thomas Brassey, became the kings of European railway contracting. They extended the French railway system and constructed railways in Belgium, Italy, and Spain.

Mackenzie was so successful and so much in demand that he had a house and offices in Paris as well as Liverpool. Sadly, he contracted gangrene, had his left foot amputated, and died in 1851. Why the pyramid? People say that he was an inveterate gambler, and the pyramid was built so that his corpse could be buried sitting upright at a card table with a winning hand. This is a myth. Mackenzie was buried in 1851 in the normal recumbent position. The pyramid was not put up until 17 years later, by his brother, who inherited the contracting business and ended up a millionaire. The pyramid shape needs no explanation: the Egyptian style was considered especially suitable for tombs and cemetery buildings.

Address St Andrew's Place, 5E Rodney Street, Liverpool L1 9ED | **Getting there** 10-minute walk from Central station | **Tip** Brian Epstein, the first manager of the Beatles, was born in 1934 across the road at 4 Rodney Street, then a private nursing home.

85___Quaker Burial Ground

A secret garden transformed into an urban oasis

An inconspicuous gate fringed with ivy opens onto a narrow passage. It leads to a walled garden surrounded by shady trees, with rows of gravestones on either side of a central pathway. This was the burial ground for Liverpool's Quakers, after interments in their city-centre cemetery were forbidden because of concerns about public health. The earliest grave is dated 1861; it marks the death of a five-year old boy, one of many children buried here. The headstones, whether for adults or children, are simple and low, all the same size and type of stone: everyone is equal in death. The visual consistency contributes to the restful atmosphere, quite different from the jumble of styles common in other cemeteries. The inscriptions are also uniform, with months numbered rather than named, because the Quakers disliked references to paganism.

The cemetery is half the size it once was: in 1906, part of the land was sold, including the site of the meeting house and the frontage to the main road. A new meeting house was built, but the cemetery became marooned between building plots without a proper entrance. The meeting house burned down in 1977 and the use of the site declined, although urns are still occasionally placed in the columbarium and ashes scattered.

In 2013, a small group of dedicated volunteers came together and began to clear the garden, by then overgrown. Gradually, they have been transforming it into a haven for wildlife and a place for contemplation, very much in keeping with Quaker ideas. They have planted flowers, fruit trees, and herbs, made a pond and brought in beehives and bird boxes. There is no water or power supply; the only concessions to convenience are a new garden shed, a chemical toilet, and a few tables where the gardeners can sit and enjoy their lunch break before continuing their peaceful work of weeding and planting.

Address Arundel Avenue, Liverpool L 17 2AT (enter via gate to left of No. 93) | **Getting there** Bus 80 or 80A from Liverpool One bus station to Sefton Park, York Avenue | **Hours** Sun 1:30pm–4pm | **Tip** Three exceptional late Victorian churches, St Clare's on Arundel Avenue, the Unitarian Church on York Avenue, and St Agnes's on Buckingham Avenue, are all within a short distance. They can be visited by appointment or on Heritage Open Days every September.

86 Queensway Tunnel

An engineering masterpiece in the Art Deco style

A behind-the-scenes tour of the Queensway Tunnel provides a remarkable insight into what was the longest underwater tunnel in the world when it opened in 1934. The tour, which begins at the George's Dock Ventilation Tower, takes you down below the river to explore the construction of the tunnel and learn how it operates today.

After the pneumatic drills were first set in action by Princess Mary in December 1925, 1,700 men worked over the nine years it took to remove 1.2 million tons of rock, clay, and gravel from beneath the river to create the void. Sir Basil Mott, the engineer, was an expert in mining, and designed the tunnel as a circular tube, of which the lower half was originally planned to house an electric tramway. When construction started there was little experience of ventilating long road tunnels, and it was only after drivers sitting in a traffic jam in the Liberty Tunnel in Pittsburgh passed out one day in 1930 that engineers realised a drastic rethink of the electrically powered ventilation system was needed. As a result, six large ventilation towers were erected, and the architect Herbert J. Rowse was brought in to design them.

The George's Dock Ventilation Tower is a masterly exercise in streamlined Art Deco design, with fine sculptures symbolising the age of the motor car: one depicts a motorcyclist wearing goggles. Within the building, visitors can see the enormous fans which force fresh air into the tunnel and take foul air out. Although their motors have been periodically replaced, the original fans remain in use. The control room, with its banks of manual switches and dials is also unchanged, but a small computer now does the job. The tour continues down to the roadway and below it, and includes a view of the latest addition: seven refuge stations, each of which will hold 180 people and basic supplies should an emergency arise.

Address George's Dock Building, George's Dock Way, Liverpool L 3 1DD, Tel +44 1513304504, www.merseytunnels.co.uk, tours@merseytravel.gov.uk | **Getting there** 5-minute walk from James Street station | **Hours** Tours: Tue–Thu 5pm, Sat 10am; tour lasts 2–3 hours; booking essential | **Tip** Overlooking the traffic at the main entrance to the tunnel in Old Haymarket are life-sized bronze statues of King George and Queen Mary.

87_River Wall

Cyclopean stonework on a heroic scale

For Ramsay Muir, Liverpool's most celebrated historian, the "vast sea wall as solid and enduring as the Pyramids" was "the most stupendous work of its kind that the will and power of man have ever created." It is here, he urged his fellow citizens, that the romance of the city can best be felt. If that is so, the best place to feel it is at the windswept marine parade on the western side of the Albert Dock, where the power and resilience of the river wall is expressed through its sublime masonry construction.

The designer was the Yorkshireman Jesse Hartley, who trained as a mason and became the city's dock engineer from 1824 to 1860. He demanded the finest granite from the Dock Board's Scottish quarries, which he used in conjunction with sandstone to resist the forces of the tidal currents and stormy seas. Hartley's response to the way that water moves is beautifully engineered in the sweeping bull-nosed setbacks of the granite wall which protects the two sets of river steps. His understanding of quayside operations can be seen at the river entrance into the Albert Dock complex. Here the coping stones on the island between the two passageways curve upwards to give warning of the edge and provide a foothold for seamen handling hawsers in wet weather.

Hartley also insisted on superlative standards of craftsmanship, perfecting the art of cyclopean masonry, the technique used by the ancient Greeks for the walls of Mycenae and Tiryns. This involved irregular pieces of granite fitted very closely together like a jigsaw puzzle, with some of the stones, up to 1.8 metres deep, providing stability. Such a method minimized waste and since labour was cheap, it was an economical as well as robust form of construction.

Greek historians thought the Mycenaeans had engaged the mythical Cyclops to build their fortresses, but Hartley had no need of giants, such was his constructional genius.

Address River wall west of Albert Dock, Liverpool L3 4AA | **Getting there** 10-minute walk from James Street station; 5-minute walk from Liverpool One bus station | **Tip** Jesse Hartley's Albert Dock is the architectural climax of Liverpool's waterfront, and a visit to the Tate Gallery, no matter what exhibitions are in progress, will lift the spirits.

88__Rolling Stone

Six tons of marble that move with miraculous ease

Underneath the modern Metropolitan Cathedral is a hidden but magnificent space. Its lofty vaulted halls and chapels, built of purple brick with granite dressings, breathe an atmosphere of solemn mystery. Off one of the halls is the Chapel of the Relics, where the archbishops of Liverpool are buried.

The doorway to the chapel is sealed with a thick slab of creamy travertine, pierced with holes in a cross-shaped pattern. When the door is opened, it is revealed to be circular in shape: although it weighs six tons, it rolls effortlessly sideways into a slot in the wall, and rolls back to close the chapel. This wondrous device, designed with perfect balance, recalls the tomb of Christ, sealed with a stone that was miraculously rolled back by the angel of the Resurrection.

The ingenuity is typical of its architect, Sir Edwin Lutyens. For years, the Catholics of Liverpool had dreamed of having a cathedral of their own, and in 1929, they asked Lutyens to design one. His scheme was approved by the Pope and construction began in 1933, but World War II brought work to a halt. Lutyens had planned a gigantic building, twice the area of St Paul's and with a dome taller than St Peter's; he imagined that, like the cathedrals of old, it would take two centuries to be completed. By the time work was stopped, 4 million bricks and 40,000 cubic feet of granite had been laid, and 70,000 tons of earth had been excavated, but only the crypt, which occupies a fraction of the footprint of the whole cathedral, had been built.

By the 1950s, the cost of completing the building, originally estimated as £3 million, had risen to £27 million. Lutyens' vision was glorious but utterly impractical. A scaled-down version was attempted, but even this proved unrealisable. Reality broke through in the 1960s, and "Paddy's Wigwam" (the present cathedral, designed by Frederick Gibberd) opened in 1967.

Address Metropolitan Cathedral of Christ the King, Mount Pleasant, Liverpool L3 5TQ, Tel +44 1517099222, www.liverpoolmetrocathedral.org.uk | **Getting there** 15-minute walk from Lime Street station; CityLink bus from Liverpool One bus station to Hope Street; bus 79 from Queen Square bus station to top of Brownlow Hill | **Hours** Cathedral: Mon–Sun 7:30am–6pm; Crypt: Mon–Sat 10am–3:30pm | **Tip** Lutyens' meticulously detailed wooden model of his cathedral is on display at the Museum of Liverpool (Liverpool Waterfront, Pier Head).

89__Roman Standard

The budgie on a stick

With public sculptures becoming bigger and more attention seeking, it was refreshingly subversive of Tracey Emin to make one that is deliberately hard to see. Named *Roman Standard*, it is a tiny bird resembling a sparrow perched on top of a bronze pole 4 metres high. Hiding behind the railings in front of the Oratory, the small, temple-like building near the Anglican cathedral, it is almost invisible unless caught in the sunlight.

Roman standards were symbols of military strength carried by soldiers. "My *Roman Standard*," wrote Emin, "represents strength but also femininity. Most public sculptures are a symbol of power which I find oppressive and dark. I wanted something that had a magic and an alchemy, something which would appear and disappear and not dominate. I have always had the idea that birds are the angels of this earth and they represent freedom." She also intended it to be a response to the Liver Bird.

When *Roman Standard* was installed, a storm of disapproval broke out, partly because it was funded by the BBC as a contribution to Liverpool's year as Capital of Culture (some felt this was an inappropriate use of the licence fee), but also because it was "something you need a pair of binoculars to see," as one objector put it, entirely missing the point. When asked what kind of bird it was, Emin caused further derision by quixotically remarking, "It vaguely resembles a swift, but then it could be a starling." It quickly became known as "the budgie on a stick" and has been paid the dubious compliment of being stolen and returned twice. The commission had an unexpected side benefit as, when visiting the site, Emin ventured inside the Anglican cathedral for the first time, resulting in a second work for Liverpool. Inside the cathedral, above the west door, is her handwritten message, "I felt you and I knew you loved me" reproduced in giant pink neon.

Address St James Mount, Liverpool L 1 7AZ | **Getting there** 15-minute walk from Central station; CityLink bus from Liverpool One bus station to Upper Duke Street | **Tip** Not far away is 62 Rodney Street, where the prime minister W. E. Gladstone was born, in 1809.

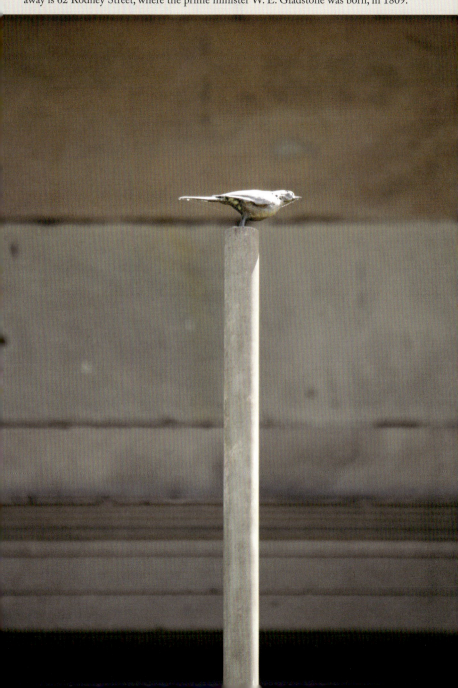

90__Salammbo

Erotic or artistic?

When the Sunlight Soap magnate Lord Leverhulme began to collect art, he used it to advertise soap. The artists were not best pleased, but Leverhulme saw a commercial message in their pictures of happy children and women in white dresses: buy my soap and you will be morally as well as physically clean. Later he decided to open a public gallery for his collection in Port Sunlight, the village he had built for his factory workers: he believed that their minds would be uplifted and their lives enriched by exposure to art.

How then did he come to buy *Salammbo*, a marble sculpture of a naked lady sensually caressing a gigantic bronze snake? (She was a priestess of ancient Carthage, from a novel by Gustave Flaubert). He also acquired the equally suggestive *Leda and the Swan* by the same sculptor, the Frenchman Maurice Ferrary. Another French sculpture by Clovis Delacour shows Andromeda tied to a rock, writhing in agony (or is it ecstasy?) at the approach of a dragon. Most of the works of art in the gallery are utterly respectable, but a few continue the theme: beautiful women are entwined with snakes in Lord Leighton's painting *The Hesperides*, while Alma-Tadema's naked Roman lady relaxing in the baths holds something resembling a vibrator. It is actually a bronze scraper, rendered with impeccable archaeological authenticity, and used by the Romans to remove oil and sweat from the skin.

Did Leverhulme, respectably married to a home-loving housewife, find these works of art titillating? Or did he consider that "high art" was above such considerations? He left no clues. The female nude was generally regarded as acceptable in an artistic context, but what of the provocative combination of naked female flesh with phallic snakes or long-necked dragons? The gallery prides itself on representing the personal taste of one man, but here is a fascinating strand in Lord Leverhulme's personality that no one has yet explained.

Address Lady Lever Art Gallery, Port Sunlight Village, Wirral CH62 5EQ, Tel +44 1514785136, www.liverpoolmuseums.org.uk/ladylever | **Getting there** 5-minute walk from Bebington station | **Hours** Daily 10am–5pm, closed Dec 24 from 2pm, Dec 25–26, and Jan 1 | **Tip** Go for a walk round Port Sunlight Village, and then learn about its history in the excellent Port Sunlight Museum, not far from the gallery.

91 — Ship and Mitre

For serious beer drinkers

The Ship and Mitre has the largest selection of hand-pulled beers on Merseyside, and serves more than 200 draught and bottled beers from around the world. Here you will find Belgian strong ales at 11 percent alcohol, German dunkels and wheat beers, Hitachino Nest Ale from the Kiuchi brewery in Japan, Siren's Liquid Mistress ("mysterious, seductive, and disarming"), and the Liverpool-based Mad Hatter Brewing Company's Nightmare on Bold Street. There is also an unusual range of ciders and perries. Craft beers are currently on the up, and the Ship and Mitre has an ever-changing selection to tempt the serious drinker.

The pub dates from the mid-1930s and retains its cream-tiled Art Deco façade. Its name combines two previous titles – the Flagship and the Mitre. The public bar was remodelled in the 1970s to give one the feel of being below decks on a sailing ship, but the upstairs function room is original and more like being aboard the Cunard liner *Queen Mary*. Weekly events include darts night on Monday, the "Sci-Bar" on the first Tuesday of the month, when a boffin will lead a discussion on matters of current scientific research while everyone enjoys a drink, and "Scouse on the House" on Wednesday. The pub also hosts its own beer festivals, including ones featuring German and Belgian ales; and there are other events such as music gigs and model-railway shows. Traditional pub food is served at lunchtime and in the evening, with a staple menu of burgers, butties, and the famous Peninsula pies.

The Campaign for Real Ale gives Ship and Mitre the accolade Pub of Excellence, and it has won their Pub of the Year award on several occasions. If you favour a pub without music, with no fruit machines, no television showing football matches, and no frills, just a mind-boggling array of quality cask and bottled beers, then the Ship and Mitre will not disappoint.

Address 133 Dale Street, Liverpool L 2 2JH, Tel +44 1512360859, www.theshipandmitre.com |
Getting there 5-minute walk from Lime Street station or Moorfields station | **Hours**
Mon−Wed 10am−11pm, Thu−Sat 10am−midnight, Sun 11am−11pm | **Tip** The pub has
a beer shop nearby, Ship in a Bottle (45a Whitechapel), selling a huge range of bottled beers
(Mon−Sat 10am−6pm, Sun noon−5pm).

92   Sodality Chapel

A glimpse of heaven

The Sodality Chapel was designed to lift the eyes and hearts of the faithful heavenwards. Almost a church in itself, it was built in 1887 in the then fashionable district of Everton, as an addition to the Jesuit church of St Francis Xavier, which had opened 40 years earlier. Attended by wealthy Catholics, the parish was famous for its choir, which was said to draw "hundreds of Protestants to hear the truths of our holy religion." By the early 20th century, however, Everton had become a working-class area, occupied by poor Irish immigrants, and the church adapted, becoming the spiritual centre of the deprived community; in the 1930s, it had the largest population of any Catholic parish in the country.

Circumstances changed again after the war. Slum clearance meant the displacement of the residents to other districts, and the area fell into decline. At a low point in the 1980s, the archdiocese was prevented from demolishing the church only by a national campaign. Today this magnificent church is linked to Liverpool Hope University, which has converted the former Jesuit College buildings alongside as a second campus.

The sumptuous Sodality Chapel, with its soaring shafts of Purbeck marble supporting a polygonal vault, is the highlight of the church. Designed by Edmund Kirby, it houses the richly decorated altars of the devotional and charitable lay associations, or sodalities. In the chancel is the altar of the Annunciation with the Virgin and Child adored by 17 Jesuit saints. Within the iron screens to each side are sensitive reliefs by Conrad Dressler in the style of the 15th-century Italian sculptor Donatello. Dressler also worked for the Della Robbia Pottery (see p. 84). Opposite is the elaborate Bona Mors altar with a marble triptych. The chapel was renamed St Mary of the Angels and St Joseph after two parishes that closed in 2001, enabling St Francis Xavier's to survive.

Address St Francis Xavier, Salisbury Street, Liverpool L 3 8DR, Tel +44 1512981911, www.sfxchurchliverpool.com | **Getting there** 20-minute walk from Lime Street station; buses from Queen Square bus station: 21 to Everton, Brunswick Road; 12 or 13 to Shaw Street | **Hours** Open every morning except Wed; Mass: Sun 10:15am, Mon, Tue, Fri, and Sat noon | **Tip** Alongside St Francis Xavier on Shaw Street is a recently restored terrace of grand Georgian houses, typical of Everton at the time the church was built.

93__ Southport Pier

… but where's the sea?

With its promenade, floral gardens, casino, and healthy fresh air, Southport is the classic seaside resort. All it lacks is the sea. At 1.75 kilometres in length, the pier is the second longest in Britain, but when you reach the end, the Irish Sea is still only a line on the horizon.

Southport is famous for its principal thoroughfare, Lord Street, which is lined with elegant gardens and arcades. The future Napoleon III stayed in the resort between 1846 and 1848. He was said to have been so impressed that when he became emperor he instructed Haussmann to remodel Paris with similarly wide boulevards.

The pier leads off from the promenade, the town's other main street, just opposite the huge statue of Queen Victoria, during whose reign the resort was created. Circumnavigate the vintage Golden Gallopers carousel, and you will find yourself on the boardwalk that skims across the Marine Gardens with its boating lake, past the Ocean Plaza shopping centre, and then over the sands, which are scattered with gleaming razor shells. If you don't want to walk all the way to the end of the pier, you can take the tram.

In 1860, when the pier was built, the sea came much closer to the shoreline and steamers berthed alongside, bringing holiday-makers from Liverpool. Designed by James Brunlees, it was the first pier where pressurised water was used to drill holes into the sand for the cast-iron piles. As with most seaside piers it has had its tragedies – the loss of the pier head in a storm and its pavilions destroyed by fire – but when the local council applied to demolish it in 1990, it caused another kind of storm: local protests. In 2002, funds were found to restore it, with a modern pavilion and a new tramway. Even if you don't see the sea, there is plenty of birdlife to capture your attention, for the wet sands provide a rich feeding ground for migrant waders.

Address Promenade, Southport PR8 1QX | **Getting there** Train from Central station to Southport (45 min) | **Hours** July–Sept, Mon–Sun 10am–6pm; Oct–June, Mon–Sun 11am–5pm | **Tip** Stroll along Lord Street, shop in the Wayfarer's Arcade (Nos. 311–317), and stop for coffee or champagne at the Vincent Cafe and Bar (No. 98).

94__ St George's Plateau

Where people come to share their joy and grief

Every city has a major civic space, its venue for public gatherings and big events; but as with its cathedrals and international football teams, Liverpool has two. There is the Pier Head, a bracing place of arrival and departure for mariners and migrants, and there is St George's Plateau, where generations of Scousers have gathered in times of celebration, anger, and despair.

In 1911, when Liverpool was a hotbed of militant unionism, the plateau saw violent clashes between police and striking transport workers, while gunboats were moored in the Mersey. Here, vast crowds witnessed the victory parade at the end of the Second World War, in October 1945, and multitudes of cheering fans have often celebrated the homecomings of winning football teams. Twenty-five thousand people came together to mourn John Lennon's assassination in 1980; and in 2008, more than 65,000 assembled to watch Ringo Starr inaugurate Liverpool's year as European Capital of Culture by singing "Liverpool, I left you, but I never let you go," from the roof of St George's Hall.

The plateau was designed as a setting for St George's Hall and is filled with public monuments. You'll find equestrian statues of Queen Victoria and Prince Albert, and dignified bronzes of Prime Minister Benjamin Disraeli and the Crimean War general, William Earle. At the centre is the Liverpool Cenotaph, created in the form of a vast tomb with bronze reliefs by H. Tyson Smith: on one side a coffin with two groups of mourners; and on the other, ranks of nameless soldiers marching to war. It is a bleak and frank depiction of inhumanity, loss, and grief. In contrast is the Wellington Column, Liverpool's version of Nelson's Column in Trafalgar Square, with the bronze statue of the Waterloo victor aloft and scenes from his glorious battle at the base. Yet with typical Scouse irreverence it is said that the more extreme your political group is, the closer to the Wellington Column you should hold your meeting.

Address In front of St George's Hall, Liverpool L1 1RJ | **Getting there** 1-minute walk from Lime Street station | **Tip** The finest equestrian statue in Liverpool, *King George III* by Richard Westmacott, is found in an unlikely location on London Road, where it faces T. J. Hughes (No. 105), the people's emporium and bargain store.

95 St James's Gardens

A melancholy but dramatic cemetery-turned-garden

A pathway cut through rock leads steeply down into a subterranean green space, originally the quarry that provided the sandstone for the Town Hall and other Liverpool buildings. By the early 19th century, the stone was exhausted and in an act of visionary planning, the architect John Foster planted trees and laid out winding walks to transform the scarred ravine into a grand cemetery.

Foster knew how to create drama, and the broad sloping ramps he designed are still impressive, with catacombs hewn out of their sides. Up to eight burials a day took place here: processions of carriages and mourners, each led by a hearse drawn by black-plumed horses, trundled slowly down the ramps to the "city of the dead." By 1936, after more than 50,000 burials, the graveyard was full, and it was closed. Attention was focused on the new cathedral rising above, and the cemetery was abandoned to weeds, ivy, and vandals. It reopened as a public garden in the 1970s, but sadly, it was "tidied up." Monuments were dismantled, graves destroyed, and headstones laid flat.

Two buildings by Foster that survived are the Grecian cemetery chapel now known as the Oratory, and far below it the elegant circular mausoleum to William Huskisson, MP for Liverpool: he died in the first railway accident, knocked down by a train on the day in 1830 when the Liverpool and Manchester Railway opened, only a year after the cemetery was inaugurated. Many lesser citizens were also buried here; the remaining stones record the deaths of sailors lost at sea, soldiers who died far from home, and large numbers of orphan children. More recently the Friends of St James's have begun to reverse the neglect. Among their plans is the restoration of the elevated walks to the east, all that remains of the fashionable Mount Sion promenade laid out in the late 18th century along the ridge where the cathedral now stands.

Address St James Mount, Liverpool L1 7AZ | **Getting there** 15-minute walk from Central station; CityLink bus from Liverpool One bus station to Upper Duke Street | **Tip** Behind the gardens is the imposing Gambier Terrace. John Lennon and Stuart Sutcliffe lived in a flat at No. 3 when they were students at the Liverpool College of Art.

96 __ St Luke's
The bombed-out church

Seen from afar, the tall tower of St Luke's is a powerful city landmark, yet as one approaches it, there is something chilling about the blank windows through which a roofless nave can be glimpsed. In the evenings, ghostly lights are visible and muffled sounds drift out from the derelict interior. This ruin, however, is not the result of neglect or gothic fantasy, for just after midnight on May 6, 1941, an incendiary bomb hit the church, one of many casualties in the most heavily bombarded British city outside London. Within a short time the roof collapsed, the bells in the tower crashed to the ground, the stained-glass windows cracked from the heat, and the interior was consumed by flames. Following the war it was decided not to restore the building but retain it in its bombed-out state as a reminder of the city's wartime resolve.

It was a melancholy fate for this proudest of churches, designed in 1802 by the corporation surveyor John Foster and erected by his son and namesake to serve the residents of the newly built Rodney Street area. Unlike other places of worship at that time, it was built in the neo-Gothic style, and was ahead of its time for the scholarly architectural language used on its richly decorated exterior. Surrounding the churchyard, which was never used for burials, are cast-iron railings with elegant Gothic tracery.

Today volunteers maintain the building and arrange an eclectic programme of events. Street food fairs are interspersed with classic films, Qi Gong classes, Flamenco music, meditation groups, and psychometric picnics. A stage has been erected in the chancel with lighting and sound, and sometimes art performances take place. Liverpool Council has been criticised at times for neglecting its historic buildings, but St Luke's is something exceptional. It shows a highly creative approach to the use of ruins, and is a poignant remnant of the city's battle-worn past.

Address Leece Street, Liverpool L 1 2TR, Tel +44 7714328415, www.bombedoutchurch.com |
Getting there 8-minute walk from Central station | **Hours** Wed – Sun noon – 6pm, also
regular evening events | **Tip** The Roscoe Head (24 Roscoe Street) is an unspoiled traditional
pub, the only one in Merseyside to appear in every edition of CAMRA's *Good Beer Guide*
since it was first published, in 1974.

97 __ St Michael's in the Hamlet

An iron church in an iron village

From 1813 to 1815, John Cragg, owner of the Mersey Iron Foundry, built a church and five villas in a quiet rural spot near the river, naming it St Michael's in the Hamlet. Cragg was passionate about cast iron and built the hamlet to promote the use of this new material. He was already erecting an iron-framed church at Everton, but at St Michael's he and his architect partner, Thomas Rickman, went much further. Cragg's inventiveness can be seen in his 1809 patent for roofs of cast iron combined with large panels of slate. A second patent for iron-faced walls, ceilings, buttresses, turrets, and spiral stairs was illustrated with drawings of St Michael's and accompanied by a description of how the intricacies of Gothic architecture could easily be replicated through casting.

Looking at the exterior of the church today, it is hard to know what is of iron and what is not; in Cragg's time it would have been even more difficult, for the iron sheet cladding of the high plinth was originally sand-coloured to resemble stone. In fact, most of what is now painted red is iron – parapets, finials, window tracery, buttress cappings, and door surrounds – while the clerestory walls consist of bricks sandwiched between slate slabs. Once inside the church, the delicacy of the cast-iron structure, with its slender clustered columns and openwork tracery, comes as a surprise.

The five villas are grouped around the churchyard, each with cast-iron windows, architraves, and verandas. Cragg lived at Hollybank, the house on St Michael's Road with fine cast-iron gate piers. Rickman was not so enthusiastic about Cragg's obsession, remarking, "His ironwork is too stiff in his head to bend to any beauty." Yet to modern eyes it is a great success: St Michael's has grace as well as advanced technology.

Address St Michael's Church Road, St Michael-in-the-Hamlet, Liverpool L17 7BD, Tel +44 1512332008, www.stmichaels-hamlet.org.uk | **Getting there** 5-minute walk from St Michael's station | **Hours** Mar–Oct, Sat 10am–4pm; churchyard open every day | **Tip** At nearby Otterspool is Fulwood Park, the earliest and most upmarket of three 19th-century residential riverside estates.

98 __ Stanley Park

Liverpool's forgotten green lung

In the 1860s, Liverpool Corporation created a belt of parks around the rapidly expanding town for the health and leisure of its citizens. Best known is Sefton Park, situated in the prosperous southern suburbs. No less remarkable is Stanley Park, to the north. North Liverpool has always been deprived, and remains so today. In the 1870s, a local satirical magazine contrasted Stanley Park with Sefton Park, which it described as a "luxurious pleasure-ground for the currant-jelly lot," and suggested that the reason Sefton cost twice as much as Stanley might have been because only 5 of Liverpool's 64 councillors lived in the northern half of the town.

Stanley Park was designed by Edward Kemp, pupil of Joseph Paxton and superintendent at Birkenhead Park. Unlike Birkenhead, it is laid out with three complementary zones. On the higher ground is a formal garden with terraces and walks contained by a long sandstone wall with Gothic-style pavilions to rest in and admire the vista. Here, formal beds of brightly coloured flowers, beloved of the Victorians, fill the foreground. Below is a more rustic landscape intended as a neutral area of grass with mounds and clumps of trees. The third zone is a picturesque setting around a lake with islands and bridges, all connected by serpentine paths with tantalising views.

In the later 20th century, Stanley Park was neglected, with dire results. Encouraged by Birkenhead Park's successful restoration, Liverpool resolved to halt the destruction and emulate the Victorian character of Sefton Park. With funding from the nearby Liverpool Football Club, the grounds were restructured, bridges were rebuilt, fire-damaged pavilions were restored, and the great glass conservatory was reglazed and brought back into use. Now the favoured place for North Liverpool weddings, with an ace cafe, the pavilion sparkles on its hilltop site.

Address Walton Lane, Liverpool L 4 2SL | **Getting there** Bus 17 from Queen Square bus station to Anfield Comprehensive School | **Hours** Daily 6am–9:30pm | **Tip** Within Stanley Park is Anfield Cemetery. Also designed by Kemp, it is the resting place of many great Liverpudlians. South of the southern catacomb is a memorial to the victims of the 1941 blitz.

99___Sudley House

An unexpected stash of Turners

In the leafy suburbs and surroundings of Liverpool, there are many large houses, originally the homes of the enterprising merchants and shipowners who made Liverpool a great world city, but only one is open to the public.

Sudley House was built in the early 19th century for a corn merchant who became mayor of Liverpool: it was a modest villa rather than an opulent mansion. George Holt, whose family owned the Lamport and Holt shipping line – pioneers of trade with Brazil – purchased the home in 1883. His hobby was collecting paintings. He added a kitchen wing; installed stained-glass windows, mahogany bookcases, and tiled fireplaces; and redecorated the reception rooms with embossed wallpapers in shades of green to set off his pictures. Amazingly, his collection survives in the house for which it was made.

You do not have to be an expert or connoisseur to enjoy Holt's Victorian paintings. They are not grandiose gallery pictures but delightful small works, scaled for a domestic interior and full of entertaining details – bright harvest landscapes and limpid river scenes, dogs by Landseer and parrots by Stacy Marks, views of Venetian canals and exotic Spanish beauties. There are also portraits by Gainsborough, Reynolds, and Romney; languid Pre-Raphaelite maidens; and a vividly coloured biblical scene by Holman Hunt. Perhaps most unexpected in this setting is a group of masterpieces by Turner, including his dramatically atmospheric seascape, *The Wreck Buoy*. Admirers of the film *Mr. Turner* may have spotted a replica of it in the scenes in Turner's studio.

The other attractions in the house include a doll's house, toys, exhibitions of historic costumes, and a tearoom in the old kitchens. The Holts' garden is now a public park with views down to the river, and you can imagine Mr. and Mrs. Holt taking tea on their veranda and watching the ships on the Mersey.

Address Mossley Hill Road, Aigburth, Liverpool L 18 8BX, Tel +44 1514784016, www.liverpoolmuseums.org.uk/sudley | **Getting there** Bus 80 or 80A from Liverpool One bus station to Mossley Hill station, then a 15-minute walk | **Hours** Daily 10am–5pm, closed Dec 24 from 2pm, Dec 25–26, and Jan 1 | **Tip** Pi (104–106 Rose Lane), a 10-minute walk from Sudley House, serves delicious gourmet pies and an extensive range of world beers.

100 Superlambanana

The new Liver Bird?

In 2008, Liverpool was awash with Superlambananas – 125 of them. Designed and decorated by local artists, children, and community groups, they were everywhere, in all colours and styles – plain, striped, and flowery; they wore football strip and hard hats; one was dressed as Sgt Pepper, another as the lord mayor. It was an inspired display of Liverpool's creativity and humour, celebrating the city's year as European Capital of Culture.

The Superlambanana story started 10 years earlier, when Manhattan-based Japanese artist Taro Chiezo made a 10-centimetre-high maquette of a lamb morphing into a banana – and it was red! The tiny model came to Liverpool and four local artists created a 2-metre-high replica of it – now yellow – for Art Transpennine, an exhibition of open-air sculpture all over the North of England. Superlambanana stayed on after the rest had gone home and Liverpudlians took it to their hearts. It was shown in several places around the city; it was painted pink to raise money for breast cancer and black and white like a cow as a student prank. In the meantime, the 125 sculptures made in 2008 were sold for charity. Some are still around and a few more have been made since, including a more durable full-size version to replace the decaying original in Tithebarn Street. They pop up all over the place: one even went to Shanghai to represent Liverpool at the World Expo.

Chiezo is intrigued by cartoons, hybrids, and mutants: another of his creations is a rabbit changing into an apple. He created Superlambanana not long after the cloning of Dolly the sheep and the spread of genetically modified crops. It is a comment on the dangers of biotechnology, a cute toy but also a monster. On another level, it could be a reference to Liverpool's trade: exporting wool and importing bananas. Interpret it as you will; it is the 21st-century symbol of Liverpool.

Address In front of Avril Robarts Learning Resource Centre, 79 Tithebarn Street, Liverpool L2 2ER, www.superlambanana.eu/index.html | **Getting there** 10-minute walk from Lime Street station | **Tip** The Lion Tavern, on the corner of Tithebarn Street and Moorfields, has a well preserved turn-of-the-20th-century interior. Its neighbour, the Railway pub, is also worth visiting for the stained glass showing nearby Exchange station.

101__ Thomas Parr's House

Home of a slave trader

Thomas Parr was one of the wealthiest merchants in late-18th-century Liverpool, and his imposing house was designed to show off both his business and his social standing. The main house faces Colquitt Street and is flanked by two lower pavilions. On the right is the former carriage house and on the left the counting house, while behind, in Parr Street, is his five-storey warehouse. When built in 1799, it was on the edge of the town; across the street, there was a large pleasure garden.

Parr inherited a share in his father's successful gun-manufacturing business for the African market, but he was also a banker and a leading slave trader. He owned the huge 566-ton ship *Parr*, which was equipped to carry 700 slaves. It was reported to have been blown up off the west coast of Africa in 1798, possibly as a result of carrying gunpowder to be exchanged for slaves. Parr's business interests suggest that his warehouse was used to store iron goods for export, no doubt guns but also possibly shackles for enslaved Africans during their transport by ship.

In 1805 Parr retired and left the city to live the life of a country landowner in Shropshire, where he was described in 1840 by Charles Darwin as "an old miserly squire." Ten years later, his Liverpool house became the premises of the Liverpool Royal Institution, as recorded on the handsome porch that was added at that time. The LRI had recently been formed by a group of Liverpool merchants with the object of promoting literature, science, and the arts. Some of its founding members were also slave traders, but the driving force behind its creation was William Roscoe, a banker and Liverpool's most distinguished man of learning. It would have been fascinating to eavesdrop on their discussions within the hallowed rooms of 21 Colquitt Street, for Roscoe was a passionate abolitionist.

Address 21 Colquitt Street, Liverpool L 1 4DE | **Getting there** 8-minute walk from Central station | **Tip** You can't beat Bold Street Coffee (No. 89) for breakfast and daytime refuelling (Mon – Fri 7:30am – 6pm, Sat 8am – 6pm, Sun 9am – 5pm).

102 Tobacco Warehouse

Guess the number of bricks

When the gargantuan Tobacco Warehouse opened in 1901, with a floor area of 1.3 million square feet, it was said to be the world's largest building. In today's era of mega-buildings it still holds its place as the largest brick warehouse in the world.

The Stanley Dock, which was built 50 years earlier, had originally been enclosed by the pair of matching brick warehouses that stand to the north and south of the Tobacco Warehouse. These proved inadequate for the burgeoning tobacco trade and so the dock was partly filled in to make way for the purpose-built behemoth. Standing 14 storeys high, its construction required 27 million bricks, 30,000 panes of glass, and 8,000 tons of steel; and it was capable of accommodating 70,000 hogsheads of tobacco (a hogshead is a large wooden barrel weighing 450 kilos when packed with tobacco). With tobacco needing to rest for two or three years before being used, the building was always full and for many years was the Dock Board's most profitable warehouse.

During the later stages of World War II, Eleanor Roosevelt came here when the sixth to eighth floors were used as a field hospital by American forces. It is reported that the First Lady travelled from floor to floor in an American Army jeep, which was driven into the lift at each level.

Tobacco storage ceased in the 1980s, and since then the building has been featured in films such as *Captain America* and *Sherlock Holmes*, and the TV series *Peaky Blinders*. The ceilings are little more than head height (calibrated to the size of tobacco hogsheads) and the floor space is vast. These factors deterred potential users; but the present owners have started repairing the building. This follows their successful hotel conversion of the North Warehouse, on the other side of the Stanley Dock, and brings hope that the Tobacco Warehouse will also become a hub of activity once again.

Address Regent Road, Liverpool L3 0AN | **Getting there** 20-minute walk from Pier Head; bus 101 from Princes Parade (Liverpool Cruise Terminal) to Great Howard Street | **Tip** A 10-minute walk north along Regent Road brings you to another titanic structure, the Tate and Lyle Sugar Silo. Built in 1957 to house 100,000 tons of raw sugar, it is thought to be the largest reinforced-concrete parabolic structure in Europe.

103__ Town Hall

At the heart of the city

Few people outside Liverpool realise that its town hall is unmatched in Britain for the splendour of its civic rooms. As soon as you enter, you are swept up a spectacular staircase below the soaring dome. At the foot of the stairs are two remarkable iron stoves in the form of Doric columns, and in the pendentives of the dome are paintings idealising the heroic labour of the dock workers. The five sumptuous reception rooms at the upper level with vaulted ceilings and gilded decoration retain their original glittering chandeliers and superb Georgian furnishings.

The building has a complex history. Designed in the 1740s by John Wood, the architect of Georgian Bath, it originally had an open exchange on the ground floor. Forty years later, it was extended and altered by James Wyatt and John Foster, and then following a fire in 1795, it was reconstructed by the same team. Wyatt added the chaste neoclassical portico overlooking Exchange Flags and the elegant dome. The friezes, representing overseas trade, are carved with Africans in exotic plumed head-dresses and turbans, elephants, crocodiles, ropes, barrels, and cotton bales.

The building's political history is also full of incident. In 1775, seamen protesting about reductions in wages launched an unsuccessful cannon attack from a ship in the Mersey, while the bosses cowered inside. A Fenian group attempted to blow it up with dynamite in 1881, and there was shrapnel damage during the blitz. In more recent times, it has seen the likes of Bessie Braddock, the ardent social campaigner who fought for the poor of Liverpool, and Derek Hatton, member of the Trotskyist militant group which brought the city council to its knees. A high point occurred in 1964, when crowds occupied the streets outside to see the Beatles appear on the balcony during a reception that became known as the Night of a Thousand Screams.

Address High Street, Liverpool L2 3SW, Tel +44 1512255530, www.liverpoolcityhalls.co.uk/town-hall/whats-on/ | **Getting there** 5-minute walk from James Street station or Moorfields station | **Hours** Monthly tours; annual open days in August and September; check website for details | **Tip** Beatwear (1 Victoria Street, www.sixtiesbeatwear.co.uk) will fit you up with authentic Beatles suits, drainpipe trousers, and Cuban heel footwear.

104__U-boat Story

See inside a German submarine

"The only thing that really frightened me during the war was the U-boat peril," confessed Winston Churchill. German submarines had a devastating impact in World War II. They were Hitler's best hope for defeating Britain and he used them in the Battle of the Atlantic to prevent merchant ships from importing food, raw materials, troops, and equipment into the country from North America. Visitors will gain an understanding of the German threat at the U-boat Story, which gives an inside view of operations on board Unterseeboot-534.

The last U-boat to leave Germany, U-534, was sunk in the final days of the war. It was heading north off Denmark on May 5, 1945, when, after ignoring an order to surrender from the commander of the German forces, Admiral Dönitz, it fell victim to a Liberator bomber's depth charge. For nearly 50 years, it lay on the seabed until a Dutch salvage company brought it to the surface. In 1996, it was brought to Birkenhead, and is now exhibited at the Woodside Ferry Terminal.

To display the inner workings of the submarine to best advantage, the U-boat was sliced into four sections. Glass panels at the ends of each section provide clear views into the control centre, motor rooms, torpedo chambers, and crew's quarters. Although the interior metalwork has been corroded by salt water, the vessel and its contents are otherwise well-preserved and strongly evoke the fearful conditions that the crew had to endure.

Some of the artefacts have been moved to an adjoining display area, including one of the U-boat's two Enigma machines, used by German military services to translate messages into code. There are also weather charts, uniforms, tins of soup, board games, medical equipment, and even a cocktail shaker. The greatest enigma, however, is why the U-boat commander failed to obey the order to surrender. The decision was to bring drastic consequences.

Address Woodside Ferry Terminal, Birkenhead CH41 6DU, Tel +44 1513301000, www.u-boatstory.co.uk | **Getting there** Ferry from Liverpool Pier Head (River Explorer Cruise tickets include free entry); train to Hamilton Square, then a 3-minute walk | **Hours** Daily 10:30am–5pm, except Christmas Day, Boxing Day, and New Year's Day | **Tip** Home Coffee at Woodside Ferry Terminal is open for breakfast, lunch, and tea (daily 10am–5pm).

105__Utility

Form follows function?

Ahead of the crowd, Dick Mawdsley, Richard Skelton, and Kate Cowie first went into business together with Coffee Union, which spearheaded the revival of artisan coffee shops in Liverpool. Dick had always been an enthusiast for modern design, and in 1999, sensing that Liverpool was on the cusp of change, the trio also opened a small design shop: Utility. Since then, the boom in city-centre apartments and the arrival of chic bars and restaurants have fuelled a demand for top-quality modern interiors. Utility now has its main store at 60 Bold Street, selling furniture, lighting, and accessories by leading international designers, two smaller gift boutiques in Liverpool, and another in King's Cross, London, plus a thriving online shop with a nationwide clientele.

The Utility home store is light and airy; daylight floods the space through large windows at front and back. Mid-century classics such as chairs by Charles and Ray Eames, Arne Jacobsen, or Gio Ponti sit alongside more recent favourites by Philippe Starck or Jasper Morrison. The Scandinavian look is ever popular: a best seller is the elegantly simple Swedish shelving and storage system String, designed in 1949 and still perfect for today's interiors. Cushions covered in Nathalie du Pasquier's vibrant fabrics catch the eye, as do colourful pendant lights by Kartell, and giant floor lamps by Artemide and Flos. Accessories include unusual glassware, kitchen items, clocks, watches, and stylishly designed books.

It is difficult to resist the seductive array of products on offer in the gift boutiques: there are gift wraps good enough to frame, classy notebooks, and coloured leather satchels. You might not want to splash out on an Eames chair or a designer watch, but you won't break the bank by buying a few greeting cards, a miniature Superlambanana, or even a desk tidy in the form of another Liverpool icon, the purple wheelie-bin.

Address Utility (home store), 60 Bold Street, Liverpool L1 4EA, Tel +44 1517084192 (gift boutiques at 8 Paradise Place and 80 Bold Street), www.utilitydesign.co.uk | **Getting there** 4-minute walk from Central station | **Hours** Mon–Fri 9:30am–6pm, Sat 9am–6pm, Sun 11am–5pm | **Tip** Round the corner is R. Jackson & Sons (20 Slater Street), an old-fashioned artists supplier and picture framer, selling everything an artist could wish for.

106 Western Approaches Command Centre

Secret World War I bunker

Churchill never wrote about it, nor did Eisenhower, although they both went there frequently. For years the authorities denied its existence and it was believed that after the war they locked it up and threw away the key. But in 1993, it was opened to the public. In a maze of bomb-proofed rooms below street level, only yards from Liverpool Town Hall, is the secret communications centre set up in 1941 to protect British ships in the Atlantic. Some 400 military, naval, and communications personnel worked here on rotating shifts 24 hours a day, monitoring the movement of convoys, German aircraft, and U-boats, and coordinating British air and sea operations. You can see the ancient teleprinters and switchboard equipment which kept the centre in touch with British airfields and naval headquarters; the cypher room, where the sender of coded messages was locked in with an armed guard posted outside; and the wooden phone box for the hotline to the war cabinet rooms in Whitehall.

The core of the command centre is a double-height room with an enormous map on one wall. From a sliding ladder, Wrens marked positions on the map, while others used wooden pushers to move counters across large charts spread out on tables to pinpoint constantly changing enemy locations. The weather and the state of readiness at RAF stations were also recorded. From behind glass windows on the opposite wall, operators could see the maps and communicate with other parts of the centre, where messages were encrypted and relayed further afield; from another window on the floor above, the admiral of the fleet could also survey operations.

Although little effort has gone into presenting and interpreting the site, it nevertheless conveys the authentic atmosphere of the 1940s and the vital part Liverpool played in the war effort.

Address 1–3 Rumford Street, Liverpool L 2 8SZ, Tel +44 1512272008, www.liverpoolwarmuseum.co.uk | **Getting there** 5-minute walk from Central station | **Hours** Mar–Oct, Mon–Thu and Sat 10am–4:30pm (last admission 3:30pm) | **Tip** Learn more about the Battle of the Atlantic at the Maritime Museum (Albert Dock, Liverpool Waterfront), a short walk away.

107__Whisky Business

For connoisseurs of the amber liquid

Going to Whisky Business is a bit like Alice's Adventures in Wonderland: the normal rules of space and logic do not apply. You know it is there, but you can't find it (the clue is two whisky barrels, one on either side of a door.) The sign above the entrance says "Jenny's Seafood Restaurant," left over from the much-lamented previous occupant. Going down the steep, narrow staircase with two tiny doors at the bottom is like falling down the rabbit hole. The door straight ahead is firmly shut but the other one is open. Down some more steps, and you encounter Murph, a large man sitting in a small room. There are no windows, just bottles, lots of them. Each is tied with an Alice-style handwritten label, which you expect to say, "Drink me." In a way, they do: "Smoother than a snooker ball"; "Big plummy fruity number with subtle hints of smoke and sweetness." They are Murph's tasting notes.

Murph learned his trade behind various Liverpool bars and now fronts this unique store, selling at least 300 different whiskies, as well as rum, vodka, vermouth, gin, and tequila, plus exotica such as mescal and cachaça. The stock is constantly changing, with new releases and special issues from distilleries all over the world – rare bottles from Scotland, Ireland, Japan, India, South America, Holland, South Africa, and Sweden – mainly small labels that you wouldn't find anywhere else. You can also buy mixology accessories, glasses, and bitters.

The affable Murph will talk you through your intended purchases and might even offer a sample or two to help train your palate. He organises regular tastings in venues across the city: find out about them on Twitter or Facebook, as Whisky Business, from the same stable as Berry and Rye (see p. 36), likes to keep things discreet. On that subject, what about that closed door at the bottom of the stairs? It's another secret cocktail bar.

Address The Old Ropery, Fenwick Street, Liverpool L2 7NT, Twitter: @lplwhisky | **Getting there** 5-minute walk from James Street station | **Hours** Tue–Fri 10am–6pm, Sat noon–5pm | **Tip** The chic Ziba Restaurant at the Racquet Club in nearby Chapel Street uses fresh produce from the owner's organic farm shop outside Liverpool.

108__ White Star Line Building

Head offices of the owners of the Titanic

April 15, 1912 was a black day for the staff of the White Star Line Building when news emerged of the sinking of the company's flagship, the RMS *Titanic*. At least 90 members of the ship's crew were from Liverpool, and most were lost in the tragedy that befell the vessel on its maiden voyage. Among those Liverpudlians who survived was the company chairman, Bruce Ismay. He was criticised for escaping from the ship by climbing into one of the last lifeboats, although he first helped many other passengers into the boats.

Like most big UK shipping lines, White Star's head offices were in Liverpool, and were designed to represent the solidity and security of their vessels. Bruce Ismay's father, Thomas, founder of the company, commissioned Richard Norman Shaw, a leading architect of the day, to design the James Street building, which opened in 1898. For the exterior, Shaw adapted his earlier design for New Scotland Yard, London, using cliff-like walls of banded brick and stone and a steeply gabled elevation to the Strand, echoing the massive dockside Goree Warehouses (known as the Goree Piazzas) which stood opposite and which were destroyed in the blitz. White Star's ground-floor booking office was unprecedented in its utilitarian style, with exposed cast-iron stanchions and beams, and a fireproof ceiling of terracotta panels, looking more like a ship's engine room than luxury first-class accommodation.

This extraordinary interior was later hidden by partitioning and suspended ceilings, but was recently revealed as part of a hotel conversion. At the sixth-floor level is the Carpathia Bar and Restaurant, named after the Cunard ship that rescued all 705 survivors of the disaster. Here you can sit on the long balcony, as if on deck, and sample a "Punch Romaine," a popular cocktail on the *Titanic*, knowing that this time, the ship won't sink.

Address 30 James Street, Liverpool L2 7PS, Tel +44 1512360166, www.rmstitanichotel.co.uk |
Getting there 1-minute walk from James Street station | **Tip** At the north end of the Pier
Head is the "Heroes of the Marine Engine Room" memorial by William Goscombe John,
unveiled in 1916. Commemorating the engineers of the *Titanic*, it is an early example of a
sculpture celebrating the heroic working man.

109 __ Williamson Tunnels

The mole of Edge Hill

A labyrinth of tunnels in a forgotten corner of Liverpool has long provoked mystery. Archaeological excavations in 1995 led to the opening of a heritage centre and the gradual rediscovery of the quirky tunnels, some of which can now be visited.

Joseph Williamson was a wealthy tobacco merchant who acquired land in Edge Hill in 1805 and built houses there. The houses on Mason Street backed onto a quarry, which he partly covered with a random series of vaults to create raised gardens. The vaults formed tunnels which he then extended below the houses themselves and beyond. Work continued until Williamson's death, after which the complex of tunnels was filled in, and in time the houses were demolished.

Williamson left behind no explanation for the tunnels, no drawings, and had no family. What information there is comes from two historians, one who visited in 1845, five years after Williamson died, and another in 1916. They described the ground as completely undermined by galleries and passages, one above another, and those under Williamson's own house as being "grotesque beyond description … Dungeons carved out of the solid rock, with no light or ventilation …" and "monstrous wine bins with many stone partitions for enormous quantities of bottles; massive erections of masonry and stone benches – all apparently without the slightest objective or motive."

Williamson's purpose is assumed to have been philanthropic, for he gave work to hundreds of men in the depression that followed the Napoleonic Wars. But there are also stories about his eccentricity – paying one man to build an arch and another to demolish it, having trap doors between the rooms of his house, and keeping a wheelbarrow in his parlour. His burrowing instinct was no doubt an obsession, and with excavations by volunteers continuing, it is tantalising to know what else might come to light in this spooky underworld.

Address The Old Stable Yard, Smithdown Lane, Liverpool L 7 3EE, Tel +44 1517096868, www.williamsontunnels.co.uk | Getting there Bus 7, 7A, 14, 14B, 61, 79, or 79C from Queen Square bus station to Smithdown Lane, then a 2-minute walk | Hours 1 Oct–31 March, Thu–Sun 10am–5pm; 1 Apr–30 Sept, Tue–Sun 10am–5pm | Tip Contemporary with the tunnels is St Mary's Church on Irving Street, which has an unaltered inner-city churchyard surrounded by a charming group of Georgian houses.

110__World Cultures Gallery

Rare artefacts from all over the world

Dark in places to protect the exhibits, underappreciated – perhaps because the works on show seem exotic and unfamiliar – and under-visited compared with the rest of the museum, the World Cultures display is one of Liverpool's great experiences: astonishing, strange, beautiful, and often joyous artefacts from distant parts of the world, from peoples whose ways of life could not be more different to ours.

Objects come from Asia, Oceania, the Americas, and Africa. The Asia display begins with a Tibetan robe made of embroidered Chinese silk; you can also see sinister-looking Japanese samurai armour, fragile Bhutanese hangings, and a carved and painted Tibetan shrine made for the 13th Dalai Lama. Oceania includes extraordinary masks and figures from New Guinea, a stunning collection of Polynesian bark cloth, and Maori jewellery and clothing. From North America come moccasins, feather headdresses, Inuit carvings, and a totem pole. The most extensive section is devoted to Africa, particularly West Africa, with a group of Benin bronzes, widely regarded as among the greatest artistic achievements of African civilisation. Other highlights include ritual figures made of wood with nails hammered into them to give them special powers, a fantastical Nigerian masquerade costume, colourful masks from Cameroon, and Nigerian pottery and musical instruments.

The stories about how these objects came to Liverpool are as fascinating as the objects themselves. Many Asian works were originally owned by Liverpool shipping families involved in the China trade, and about half the African items on show were donated by one person, the former chief engineer to the Elder Dempster shipping line; many of these were given to him by traders, colonial administrators, and African chiefs. However strange and exotic these items seem, they are now an integral part of Liverpool's history.

Address World Museum, William Brown Street, Liverpool L3 8EN, Tel +44 1514784393, www.liverpoolmuseums.org.uk/wml | Getting there 5-minute walk from Lime Street station | Hours Daily 10am–5pm, closed Dec 24 from 2pm, Dec 25–26, and Jan 1 | Tip Across St John's Gardens is Doctor Duncan's pub, named after Britain's first Medical Officer of Health, with a spectacular room lined in Victorian tiles.

111 _ Ye Cracke

Tiny pub frequented by John Lennon

Ye Cracke is not everyone's idea of a perfect pub: some might call it grotty, but one man's grotty is another man's authentic. Let's get the grot over with: chipped paintwork, wobbly tables with sticky tops, and toilets that would certainly not get into the Good Loo Guide. Despite all this, it has the feeling of a genuine old-fashioned local. The boarded floors, the unplanned nooks and crannies, the beer garden, and the changing selection of real ales makes it a popular drinking haunt with a patina that no interior designer could create. It would be a tragedy if it were to be smartened up.

Ye Cracke is famous for its associations with John Lennon, who was a regular here when he was an art student. He used to drink Black Velvet, a beer cocktail made from floating stout on top of sparkling white wine. Lennon brought Cynthia, later his first wife, to Ye Cracke after meeting her at a college dance, and he also came in after learning that his mother had been killed. A plaque in the public bar commemorates the occasion in June 1960 when he and his friends Stuart Sutcliffe, Bill Harry, and Rod Murray visited the pub after a poetry reading at Liverpool University given by Royston Ellis (the paperback writer of Paul McCartney's song). Disappointed with Ellis's performance, they talked of forming a group called the Dissenters, but it never happened.

The plaque is the only thing that looks new in the otherwise timeworn interior. From a passage you can see through internal windows into the snug, lined with ancient red leatherette banquettes; it is known as the War Room and you can easily imagine crusty regulars meeting here to debate the politics of the Boer War. In the evenings, this tiny hostelry becomes so crowded that you can hear the hubbub from the street. Perhaps that is the origin of the pub's name, a Northern English and Irish word for convivial conversation.

Address 13 Rice Street, Liverpool L1 9BB, Tel +44 1517094171 | **Getting there** 10-minute walk from Central station; CityLink bus from Liverpool One to Hope Street | **Hours** Sun–Thu noon–11:30 pm, Fri–Sat noon–midnight | **Tip** Close by, in Hope Place, an enclave of attractive Georgian houses with long front gardens, the pocket-sized Unity Theatre, converted from a Victorian synagogue, continues a tradition of radical theatre.

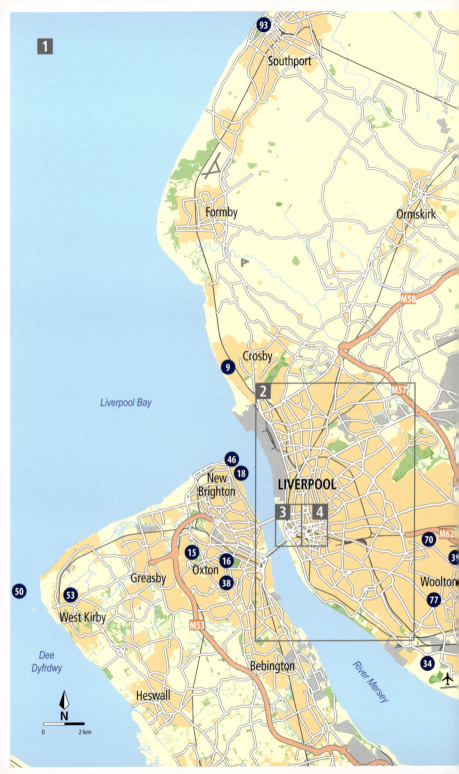

1

93
Southport

Formby

Ormskirk

M58

Crosby

9

Liverpool Bay

2

M57

46
New
18
Brighton

LIVERPOOL

3 **4**

15
Oxton
16
38

70 M62

3

Woolton

50

53
Greasby

West Kirby

77

M53

34

Dee
Dyfrdwy

Bebington

River Mersey

Heswall

N

0   2 km

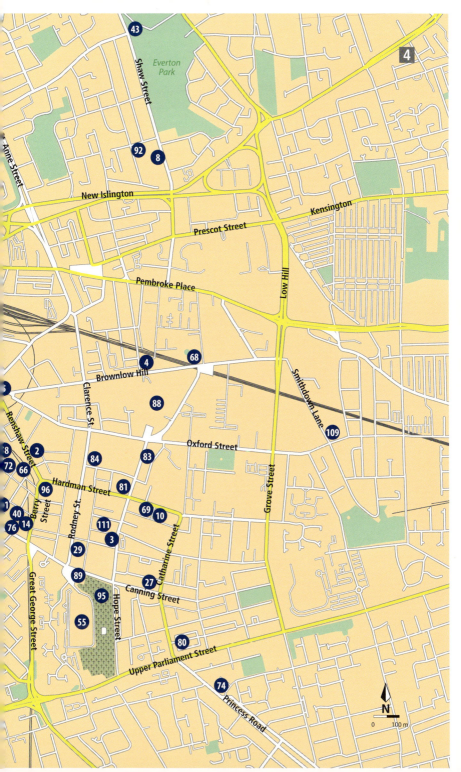

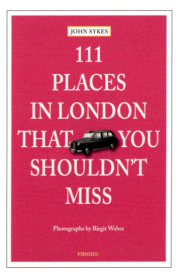

John Sykes
**111 PLACES IN LONDON
THAT YOU SHOULDN'T MISS**
ISBN 978-3-95451-346-8

London is full of strange sights. Where was a king of
Corsica buried in Soho? Which wine dealer has records
of its customers' body weight?
Can a subterranean cycle rout lead to Scotland?
And why was a high-rise block designed by James Bond's
mortal enemy?
The secret London is getting harder and harder to find.
This book takes you to 111 extraordinary and surprising
places.

Lucia Jay von Seldeneck,
Carolin Huder, Verena Eidel
**111 PLACES IN BERLIN
THAT YOU SHOULDN'T MISS**
ISBN 978-3-95451-208-9

Rüdiger Liedtke
**111 PLACES IN MUNICH
THAT YOU SHOULDN'T MISS**
ISBN 978-3-95451-222-5

Frank McNally
**111 PLACES IN DUBLIN
THAT YOU MUST NOT MISS**
ISBN 978-3-95451-649-0

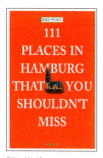

Rike Wolf
**111 PLACES IN HAMBURG
THAT YOU SHOULDN'T MISS**
ISBN 978-3-95451-234-8

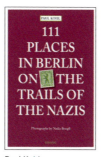

Paul Kohl
**111 PLACES IN BERLIN
ON THE TRAIL OF THE NAZIS**
ISBN 978-3-95451-323-9

Peter Eickhoff
**111 PLACES IN VIENNA
THAT YOU SHOULDN'T MISS**
ISBN 978-3-95451-206-5

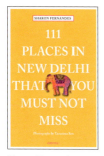

Sharon Fernandes
**111 PLACES IN NEW DELHI
THAT YOU MUST NOT MISS**
ISBN 978-3-95451-648-3

Sally Asher, Michael Murphy
**111 PLACES IN NEW ORLEANS
THAT YOU MUST NOT MISS**
ISBN 978-3-95451-645-2

Gordon Streisand
**111 PLACES IN MIAMI
AND THE KEYS
THAT YOU MUST NOT MISS**
ISBN 978-3-95451-644-5

Dirk Engelhardt
**111 PLACES IN BARCELONA
THAT YOU MUST NOT MISS**
ISBN 978-3-95451-353-6

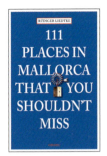

Rüdiger Liedtke
**111 PLACES ON MALLORCA
THAT YOU SHOULDN'T MISS**
ISBN 978-3-95451-281-2

Marcus X. Schmid
**111 PLACES IN ISTANBUL
THAT YOU MUST NOT MISS**
ISBN 978-3-95451-423-6

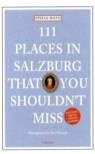

Stefan Spath
**111 PLACES IN SALZBURG
THAT YOU SHOULDN'T MISS**
ISBN 978-3-95451-230-0

Ralf Nestmeyer
**111 PLACES IN PROVENCE
THAT YOU MUST NOT MISS**
ISBN 978-3-95451-422-9

Christiane Bröcker,
Babette Schröder
**111 PLACES IN STOCKHOLM
THAT YOU MUST NOT MISS**
ISBN 978-3-95451-459-5

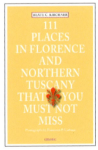

Beate C. Kirchner
**111 PLACES IN FLORENCE
AND NORTHERN TUSCANY
THAT YOU MUST NOT MISS**
ISBN 978-3-95451-613-1

Floriana Petersen, Steve Werney
**111 PLACES IN SAN FRANCISCO
THAT YOU MUST NOT MISS**
ISBN 978-3-95451-609-4

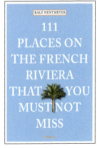

Ralf Nestmeyer
**111 PLACES ON THE
FRENCH RIVIERA
THAT YOU MUST NOT MISS**
ISBN 978-3-95451-612-4

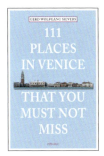

Gerd Wolfgang Sievers
**111 PLACES IN VENICE
THAT YOU MUST NOT MISS**
ISBN 978-3-95451-460-1

Petra Sophia Zimmermann
**111 PLACES IN VERONA
AND LAKE GARDA THAT
YOU MUST NOT MISS**
ISBN 978-3-95451-611-7

Rüdiger Liedtke,
Laszlo Trankovits
**111 PLACES IN CAPE TOWN
THAT YOU MUST NOT MISS**
ISBN 978-3-95451-610-0

Annett Klingner
**111 PLACES IN ROME
THAT YOU MUST NOT MISS**
ISBN 978-3-95451-469-4

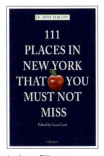

Jo-Anne Elikann
**111 PLACES IN NEW YORK
THAT YOU MUST NOT MISS**
ISBN 978-3-95451-052-8

Giulia Castelli Gattinara,
Mario Verin
**111 PLACES IN MILAN
THAT YOU MUST NOT MISS**
ISBN 978-3-95451-331-4

Mark Gabor, Susan Lusk
**111 SHOPS IN NEW YORK
THAT YOU MUST NOT MISS**
ISBN 978-3-95451-351-2

Kirstin von Glasow
**111 SHOPS IN LONDON
THAT YOU SHOULDN'T MISS**
ISBN 978-3-95451-341-3

Kirstin von Glasow
**111 COFFEESHOPS IN
LONDON THAT YOU MUST
NOT MISS**
ISBN 978-3-95451-614-8

Acknowledgements

Special thanks to: Waltraud Boxall; Patrick Higgins; John Hinchliffe; Alistair Layzell; Joseph Sharples; Julian Spalding; Felicity Crease; Robin Riley; Maureen Bampton; Bryan Biggs; Elaine Harwood; Justine Mills, Lorraine McCullough and Sue Poole; Nicola Pink and Lavinia Cooke; Michael Simon; Colin Simpson; Ingrid Spiegl; Leonie Sedman; Jayne Garrity; Alaster Burman and Dr Peter Grant; Olwen McLaughlin; Dick Mawdsley; Paul Murphy; Peter Woods; and Dr Zachary Kingdon

The Authors

Peter de Figueiredo's family has been in Liverpool for over 200 years. He trained as an architect before working for the city of Chester and for English Heritage. He has developed an unrivalled knowledge of the architecture of Liverpool and the North West, and now has his own consultancy as an adviser on historic buildings.

Julian Treuherz is an adopted Scouser. He was born in Littleborough, Lancashire, and worked in Manchester before coming to Liverpool to direct the Walker Art Gallery and the Lady Lever Art Gallery, Port Sunlight. An expert in Victorian art, he received an honorary degree from the University of Liverpool in 2009.